*Island at the End
of the World*

BERNARD GORSKY

Island at the End of the World

TRANSLATED FROM THE FRENCH BY
ALAN HOUGHTON BRODRICK

RUPERT HART-DAVIS
SOHO SQUARE LONDON
1966

Printed by Eyre and Spottiswoode Limited, at The Thanet Press, Margate for Pierre Pasquier

Contents

Note

THE *Moana* expedition was a great adventure, on the seas and under the seas, and it lasted thirty-seven months. Four men on a sailing boat conducted a series of submarine explorations while navigating round the globe. Bernard Gorsky was the leader and his companions were Pierre Pasquier, Roger Lesage and Serge Arnoux. What had appealed most to Bernard Gorsky—more than the lure of discovery, the taste for risk or the urge to be 'somewhere else' (which Steinbeck has said is for some men, including himself, an incurable malady)—was the necessity to break away from a life where he could not really find the inspiration he must have if he would satisfy his master-passion—that of writing.

Introduction

WHEN the second book about the *Moana* expedition was published in Paris, we realized that the mass of documentation brought back from our trip around the world was sufficient to provide material for a book of the 'travel album' sort. I would write the text and captions for the photographs. The thing was decided and done.

Months passed by. Then one morning I got advance copies of the book and it was with some melancholy that I flipped through the illustrated summary of three years of maritime adventure . . . the fitting out of the little boat by the banks of the Rance, the Atlantic crossing, the West Indies, the Galapagos, the unforgettable stay at Tahiti. The last photograph showed us on *Moana's* deck the day we got to Saint-Tropez, and the closing words were, 'What are we going to do now?'.

I shut the album and put it on a shelf, above one decorated with star-fish and shells gathered once by the shores of a lagoon. The din of the traffic rose from the rue Bonaparte. A passing bus shook the windows. I drew aside the curtains. A sulky fog still dulled the winter morning. The lights from the antique shops glistened on the pavement's half-melted snow. My mind went back to the Coral Sea island, rising from a sapphire blue ocean, green and thickly wooded, bordered with white sand where hermit-crabs scuttled. 'What are we going to do now?'—the irony of the phrase stabbed me to the heart.

So I sat down to examine dispassionately just what my position was. I had been fool enough to imagine I could easily readapt myself at home. But you cannot seize the freedom to range about the world and then imprison that liberty in an apartment with a thousand objects, each one of which is tempting you to set off once more on your travels. It is not easy to leave the peaceful life of far-off archipelagoes and settle down again in the vain commotion of a capital city. You cannot with impunity leave the vivifying air of the trade-winds for the poisonous miasma of a great city. It is very difficult to take your place again among that swarming mass of men of whom Jean Rostand has truly said that theirs is a lethal life. When all was said and done I did feel deeply attached to our civilization, but I had to admit that it was testing me terribly. What should I do?

Since I had been back my recent experience of a long adventure had aroused the curiosity of friends. But I soon discovered this curiosity was far from being gratuitous. For a time I rather liked, with my anecdotes and my air of strange adventure, to heighten the eccentricity expected of me, but I soon got disgusted with pandering to their credulity. So I refused to let other people dissect me: I began to dissect other people.

All, with very few exceptions, were consumed with a real longing for change, that is to say they wanted to get away from conditions which, however, made escape impossible. Escape was for them doubly imperative, both for the body infected, choked by the poison of their physical surroundings, and for the soul filled with age-old longings for Paradise Lost. Departure was an almost chemical reaction for those surviving in a world that was no doubt evolving and developing but which I had every day been less able to recognize as my own. It was dominated by the spirit of lucre and of fierce competition. Its spirituality had been diminished by the crushing forces of materialism—and it was absurdly divided against itself while threatened with atomic destruction.

How should I be different from anyone else, now that I shared the common lot?

So if I went off again, it certainly would be alone. And the mere fact that I was examining and considering this aspect of a new evasion, convinced me that I had already decided on it.

Tahiti

1767   Captain Wallis in *Dolphin* discovers the island of Otaiti, Lat. 17 South and Long. 151 West.

1768   Captain Bougainville of the French Navy in the frigate *La Boudeuse* and accompanied by the fly-boat *L'Etoile* lands at Hitaa, Otaiti.

1769   Captain Cook lands at the cape later called 'Venus' not far from Papeete Bay (Otaiti).

1773   After sailing from Peru Don Domingo Boenechea founds a Catholic mission at Tautira (Otaiti).

1789   HMS *Bounty*, commander, Captain Bligh RN, puts in at Otaiti to take on board several thousand plants of the bread-fruit tree for conveyance to the West Indies.

1797   The first Methodist missionaries arrive on board *Duff*.

1842   Melville in Tahiti.

1847   Queen Pomaré IV of Tahiti accepts a French protectorate.

1872   Pierre Loti in Tahiti.

1880   King Pomaré V, son of Queen Pomaré IV, cedes his kingdom to the French.

1888   Robert Louis Stevenson in Tahiti.

1891   Paul Gauguin in Tahiti.

1903   Death of Paul Gauguin.

1907   Jack London in Tahiti.

1958   First air-link with Tahiti.

1961   The first jet plane lands on the Faaa airstrip, Tahiti.

1962   Tahiti is proclaimed officially a 'paradise accessible to international tourism'.

1 Visa for Paradise

Two o'clock in the morning and we were already there. I had not even finished reading a book I had begun just after we had left Orly. In a sailing boat it had taken me a year to do the same trip.

Extraordinary—ever since one of the passengers made out the lights of Tahiti everyone was crazy with enthusiasm. At the magic word 'Tahiti' all the self-conscious reserve that stifles conversation between strangers disappeared. People chatted to each other from one end of the long rows of seats to the other . . . 'Tahiti, here we are, we're nearly there, hurrah, hurrah . . .' One man of about fifty took off the jacket of his Palm Beach suit, tied the sleeves around his well-developed waist, executed a few dance-steps and wriggled about up and down the corridor. Couples cuddled and some people were so moved that they had to hide their tears.

Without a bump the huge plane landed on the famous coral runway and we jostled towards the door opening on to a warm night of perfume. The part of the airport in front of us was illuminated by torches brandished by two rows of men and women dancers. The drums throbbed, the torches held high up at arms' length made a crisscross pattern, a sign of joy at the opening of the dance. All the performers were in traditional national costume. Each of us, as he reached the bottom of the gangway, received a garland of fresh, heavily-scented frangipani blossoms, as well as a kiss from one of the *parāu*-clad hostesses. The adorable softness of brown cheeks, the friendly warmth of dark eyes shining with infectious gaiety, the marvellous intimacy of a voice murmuring, '*Iora na*—Welcome to Tahiti' . . . mesmerized by all these exotic and novel impressions and almost choking with delight, our flock followed the guide to the customs-house, trailing along in front of the group of dancers.

Waved in unison with the beating of the drums the crackling torches accentuated movements executed with faultless harmony. Dancing flames shed glistening reflections on the naked bellies of the women, on their rounded shoulders and graceful arms, on the muscular chests of the men, on the golden straw of the costumes and on the helmets decorated with shells. Every face was smiling. Under eyebrows suddenly raised—the movement expressing 'good day' in Tahitian—eyes opened wide in a message of welcome and friendship.

It was intoxicating. These five score or so men and women, who knew nothing of each other except for glimpses in the jet or a few commonplaces exchanged at earlier landings, were bound together by sharing this arrival in the Promised Isle. From our world, harsh and indifferent, they had been transported to a dominion of their dreams—which were indeed transcended. None could have dared to imagine that his nameless presence could provoke such an outburst of joy.

The police and customs formalities took place in a huge sheet-iron shed and in an atmosphere of a tropical fair. Loud-speakers blared Tahitian melodies. On every side were songs, laughter, jokes. We were all over-excited. Despite his uniform an imposing Tahitian customs-man looked just as though he had stepped out of a Gauguin picture. Nothing to declare? Half-hidden behind his pile of heavy suitcases the passenger next to me shouted, 'Yes, I want to declare that I'm crazily happy'. The customs-man burst out laughing, scribbled some chalk-marks on the luggage and shoved it along. The police-man behind his window stamped a residence visa on my passport. 'Visa for Paradise', shouted the tourist behind me. 'Perhaps, if you get on all right with the *vahiné*,'[1] said the

(1) Tahitian girls.

'the poisonous miasma of a great city'
'the Coral Sea Island rising from a sapphire-blue ocean, green and thickly wooded, bordered with white sands'

policeman, and he winked and pulled a droll face. A hostess guided our party to the exit.

There, facing us, Moorea stood out under a full moon. Enormous stars threw their reflections on the lagoon's silky surface. The arrival of a taxi saved me from emotions that threatened to stifle me.

I chose an hotel on the lagoon shore, a few miles from Papeete. My bungalow was very up to date and most comfortable, a charming replica of a Tahitian cabin. It lay between the road that circles the island and the strand, near a grove of coco-palms.

The refrigerator contained a bottle of Coca Cola.

In one corner was the air-conditioning unit. The shower was shiny, with a bright plastic curtain. On a table lay a stack of luxurious writing paper. Fine coloured sheets decorated a lacquered bamboo bed. Its coverlet was of the same *paräu*[1] stuff, with bright designs, as the sunblinds. But how could one sleep? I went out on to the narrow beach and leant against a canoe.[2] I stood absorbing the beauty around me as dawn began to break over Moorea.

But the next day taught me that on this first night of dreams the gods had been too good to me. They could give me no more. They were exiled to their own realm and they came down from Drohené, their Olympus, only in the silent hours.

No bitterness poisons the thoughts of those who, on the way back from the very sources of our civilization, have to cross the noisy, crowded Athen streets to reach their hotel, or the Piraeus and their cruise-ship. The ruins of ancient Greece rise up far higher than their builders ever imagined they would—witnesses to a culture thirty centuries old, whose influence spreads ever wider over the world.

Something quite different happens in Tahiti.

---

(1) The loin-cloth of the Oceanians. (2) That is a piragua or sea-going canoe.

2 *A Letter to a Friend*

My friend,

You must excuse this indecent haste. You asked me to write to you about Tahiti, and of course I agreed. But here I am writing already. Certainly you didn't expect a letter so soon. You must have thought me lost in a world of delights; but I am only lost.

The mere fact that this letter (with its pretty stamp of the *pterois volitans*—the fish of death—amazingly wiped out at Papeete) will get to you within fifty hours after I have put it on the Jet, reveals my mistake in wishing to live again our *Moana* past. To tell the truth my journey was just a ghost-chase. Its ghosts that I am up against. Don't think I'm embittered or disillusioned or that I am just handing out stories to console you, knowing how much you'd like to be in my place—or rather how much you'd have liked to come with me. Things here have changed, that's all.

Tahiti is diminishing. We don't come to look for ourselves here, but that's all we find. It doesn't work the other way round. I know that, and I knew it before I started out . . . but starting out is something in itself!

When we got here in *Moana*, Touamotou had been our last landfall and we had been sailing the oceans for a year since we had left Saint-Malo. Not a franc on board, but we spent seven wonderful weeks. We had come from the sea and we would go off on the sea. Tradition. We were the kings of the island. There was a wonderful way of hallowing Tahiti at Tahiti and that was to put the government in the hands of sailors. The chief of the national navy, absolute ruler. Come by ship, by sailing-ship for preference, find some way—swim here, good for the health. . . .

I am talking really like a conservative, a reactionary, an old Southerner who understands nothing about democracy and who is jealous of his property: 'dreams, escape, meditation'. Do you remember M used to call me the 'submarine wandering jew'? He didn't know how right he was. My wandering will go on, maybe Touamotoua, perhaps the Marquisas, possibly elsewhere.

I am sending you the *parāu* and the Bora-Bora dance costume as I promised, and also the *tamouré* records. I can imagine you from here with your *vahiné popaa*, as white as an aspirin (but very pretty), in your studio . . . the gramophone . . . make a punch (rum, syrup, lemon, cinnamon, ice) and drink my health, as I am drinking to yours outside the bar overlooking the lagoon (that's why there's a stain on the paper). Ever yours . . .

Several weeks passed. I was baffled, confused, chasing a past that ever eluded me. I drove about Papeete in a hired car passing up and down before the string of yachts at the quayside where seven years before my sailing-boat had been moored. I recognized nothing and no one recognized me. My search for old memories became positively morbid. I must get away.

I had been fascinated by the story of a sailor who had visited the Wallis Islands. He described a sort of medieval Polynesia, a survival of those times whose disappearance is so to be deplored in Tahiti. It was very hot there. The islands had been until lately completely isolated, but recently a monthly air service had been started.

'Is it anything like Tahiti?'

'No, not at all.'

He poured a little more whisky into our glasses set on a square table. He chinked his glass against mine and as he drank stared fixedly at the stream of cars and scooters rattling and spluttering along the quay.

'No, most certainly not anything like Tahiti.'

19

The island of Tahiti has an area of four hundred and two square miles. At its longest it does not exceed forty miles or so, and its breadth is about twenty-five miles. The population is not more than thirty thousand. Yet, tiny as it is, this world-famous island is fast becoming a tourist shrine, a 'high place'.

How and why did Tahiti acquire a celebrity which is maintained even by efforts made to dissipate misunderstandings? Marvellous natural beauty? Yes, that is true and beyond all description. Tahiti is wonderfully lovely. Still, some people might think other places equal, if not superior in beauty. Is it the easy manners and customs, the legend of the *vahiné* giving herself at the first invitation—if, indeed, she waits for an invitation? Supposing that this may sometimes be true, it is not enough, it never was enough. No, the fame of Tahiti has been due to its civilization, more inspired by Christian principles than any other which has ever existed. It was a civilization based on the most genuine of Christian precepts—that of offering. What Captain Wallis found in 1767 was much more than a hitherto unknown and mountainous island inhabited by a carefree people—it was the revelation that the rest of the world was not Christian. Our own civilization, culturally rich though it is, cannot create happiness, but we undertook to transform a people whose only culture was based on the cult of happiness. I got to Tahiti among those who witnessed the last act of a classical tragedy.

Before the beginning of the Tourist Age, that is to say barely fifteen years ago, maybe even a little less, among the chosen few who reached Tahiti—civil servants, doctors, pensioners, artists, navigators—there were some who fell into no definite category other than that marked by a contempt for what elsewhere than in Tahiti are known as worldly possessions (the owners of which, it must be said, repaid the contempt with interest). Some of these unclassified people, still standing upon their dignity, found jobs within the island's primitive economy. Others became what the Tahitians humorously called 'banana tourists' because they seemed complacent enough living on bananas, which in those days cost nothing at all.

When these men arrived a paternal government asked nothing of them but a guarantee of about sixty thousand francs, in those days the price of a ticket back to Europe, steerage class, on a Messageries Maritimes ship. This journey the Governor would only request them to undertake in cases of grave and repeated misconduct and riotous behaviour. The little European colony was so strongly influenced by local customs that not only did it treat such tropical beatniks and beachcombers with a total absence of prejudice but they were invited to the *tamaaraa* (banquets) held every evening and were offered a roof for as long as they liked when they did not want simply to dream under the stars. In fact, everything was fine for the banana tourist in those days that are no more.

Nowadays there is no time for banana tourists; only for tourists. A refusal to adapt oneself to the new economy, that of tourism, either by living on it or keeping it going, means social ruin—the inadaptable, the failure. Present society looked with contempt on the last of these apprentice Robinson Crusoes who had most imprudently turned up in a place where there was no more room for them, illogically persisting in their out of date dreams. Great projects are set up by clear-sighted, ambitious and energetic men working with inter-national business groups—projects for garages, car parks, bowling alleys, big hotels, casino and even an electric railway. No one in Papeete or in the districts (*quartiers*) foresaw to what giddy heights land-prices might rise. The soil of the most hospitable people in the world had become the prey of speculators.

Before this new disease had been imported into Tahiti (and it will soon infect all Polynesia) for the inhabitants the words 'riches', 'money', 'profit' had no meaning. 'Commerce' could not be translated into Tahitian except as far as it referred to human relations. The sixteen letters of the Tahitian alphabet were used first of all to spell out words of welcome and fraternity, words of songs celebrating love, bountiful nature, the acceptance of all and everything as coming from the gods. The sharing of possessions, an inaptitude for any sort of calculation, and complete solidarity were as much a part of Tahitian existence as the *maaramu* (trade winds) that rocked the coco-palms or Moana the Mother (the word probably means 'the sea that is our mother') rich in fish and mother-of-pearl. Trade was in the hands of the taciturn Chinese or of the representatives of a few European firms who let themselves sink into the state of *aïta péa péa* (which one might translate as, 'it doesn't matter').

We have dumped on Tahiti, on a huge scale, the weapons of our ideology—objects. Create needs and through them become indispensable. A thousand manufactured products exercise their fascinating power. Through the Papeete streets whizz the convertibles, the *vahiné's* dearest dream, the decisive evidence of conquering vigour. Everything matters. *Aïta péa péa* means nothing. I was hardly surprised to hear a rich Tahitian, and a sharp business man, say to me, 'I went to France last year. A magnificent country. And land is really cheap!'

Symbols of Tahiti in the Tourist Era are those small baskets of wild oranges that are hung up by the roadside. No one watches over them. For anyone fascinated by the stories of Polynesian customs we read in the books of nineteenth-century navigators, nothing seems more charming than these wild fruits offered to you; it is when you get near and stretch out your innocent hand to the containers of plaited palm-leaf that you discover in them a little cardboard ticket with the price, one hundred and eighty CPF francs (ten new French francs). No amount of reasoning can soothe the childish disappointment. You see with pitiless clarity just how much you had dreamt of things that you don't do yourself.

There will come the day anticipated—especially by the bankers—when the Tourist Era will produce a sort of balance between those who offer a good time without any secrets at all, and those who pay for it. No one believes it any more, but on the other hand no one is fooled. The myths have been buried long since: no one complains for they have been forgotten. That time will perhaps be one of prosperity, most probably of mediocrity, certainly of boredom. Our present age is that of cruelty.

One of the most cruel jokes of the Tourist Era turns on a rather feeble but ferocious pun . . .

From time to time a magnificent liner will bring to Papeete roads hundreds, sometimes thousands of cruising American tourists. They all seem to be aged—very old indeed. The gigantic outline of the ship at the quayside dominates the whole port, and Papeete's streets become a promenade for aged men and women. Following what is thought to be proper wear in the tropics all these old people disguise themselves as babies when they totter along the famous eight hundred yards of curio shops, office-buildings and tourist-agencies, and the sole and only café with a terrace giving on the lagoon. Some visitors even venture as far as the *rue Gauguin* and the Chinese stores near the fish-market. All patiently join the interminable queue at the window where the *poste restante* mail is handed out in the modern and monumental Post Office.

The liner is called *Mariposa*. It is nicknamed *Menoposa*. Not very witty? Well, it may have more point when you know that there is a morgue on board. Indeed, some of those grotesque babies, having at last made their dreams come true, having seen the Cythera of the Southern Seas, are so old that they go home in a refrigerator.

3 Wallis

Nine hundred and twenty miles north-east of New Caledonia lies the Wallis archipelago—so called from the name of the English navigator who discovered it in 1767—consisting of the main island of Ouvéa, measuring twelve miles by four, which is surrounded by smaller islets, all in a lagoon fringed and protected by a barrier reef of coral. The climate is typically equatorial and the archipelago is situated in a region of cyclone formation. The rainfall reaches 118.5 inches on the slopes exposed to the trade-winds, but this side of the island contains the most houses since the air is cooler than elsewhere. During the cyclone season—from October to March—both heat and humidity are very great. The population, which is entirely Catholic by religion, is of Polynesian stock. In addition to the six thousand natives, there is a number of Europeans consisting of thirty-five missionaries, civil servants or soldiers. There are no settlers. Authority over the Wallisians is exercised by a 'king' and his ministers who reside at Mata Utu, the administrative centre. A French protectorate was established by treaties concluded in 1887 and 1888, but after a referendum held on 27th December 1959, the status of the archipelago was changed and it became a French Overseas Territory. Ninety-five per cent of the electors voted in favour of the new régime. After the referendum a Provisional Assembly was established in order to prepare the organization of the Territory.

THE meal was ending. Outside, the night rain was spattering on the broad palm-tree roof. Damp heat filled the great room whose walls were adorned with turtle-shells, sharks' jaws and sea-shells. Mosquitoes buzzed round the incandescent lamps. Benjamin Brial, my host, turned his head towards a maid who was standing motionless in the window-recess. She at once came forward to clear the table. Her very wide, bulging fore-

'the Americans had a base on Wallis during the last war'
overleaf: 'bare-back on half-wild horses'
overleaf: 'I noticed the high, broad forehead characteristic of Malay women'

head was tattooed, as were her arms from wrists to elbows. She was wearing one of those dresses whose odd appearance had struck me that morning when I got off the plane. All the women I caught sight of through the pelting rain wore similar garments of antiquated cut. You would have said they were Breton dresses of a by-gone age, made out of a thin velvet with a dull lustre showing against a background of bright red. Absolute deference and submission were expressed by the attitude of this tall, well-built girl. She seemed about fifteen years of age. She kept her eyes lowered and bowed slightly each time one of her movements led here near her master.

'You see,' he said, 'that's how a servant behaves here. I've often told her to be a little more at ease, not to be so formal, but whatever I may say, she'll never change. For her I am the son of the former Queen, almost a god. She was brought up like that.'

You could read intelligence and vivacity in Benjamin Brial's face. He was a descendant of the royal family, the leader of the Opposition, and the man without whom I could do nothing and, indeed, learn nothing here. He had studied at Nouméa College and spoke perfect French, whereas, as he told me, neither the reigning king, nor his ministers, nor the village headmen, nor, with very few exceptions, anyone on the island, knew a word of French.

Brial was deeply attached to his own people and had made himself the champion of all measures which might free them from their ignorance and apathy. His ideal was a social progress which should not corrupt the typically Wallisian traditions and customs. Such precious and unique possessions should be preserved while everywhere else in the Pacific, Polynesian manners and customs were being forsaken or treated with contempt by the younger generation. But the essential thing was to liberate his people from constraints and controls which reduced human beings to the condition of serfs.

'Things are going to change now?'

inside: 'the incredible link between the Polynesians and a monument of medieval faith'
inside: 'Polynesians, discovered only in the eighteenth century'
'the men were huge'

'Maybe, but it'll take a long time. For quite trivial offences everyone and anyone, it doesn't matter who he is, gets fined. And no small fine either—a pig.'

Indignation stifled Brial's voice.

'But that really doesn't seem possible.'

'Do you want an example? Take this referendum—which after all was the first act of a democratic sort. Well, in one village, the headman, who's got the rank of minister, decided that the polling-booths should be open only in the morning. One poor devil of a fisherman who did not know about the ruling turned up in the afternoon. No one would listen to his explanations or his excuses. He was fined a pig, and you know that a pig is often all a Wallisian owns in the world.'

'What did the fisherman do?'

'He paid. He knew what would have happened to him if he refused.'

'What?'

Brial made a meaningful gesture.

'He'd have been beaten up.'

'More than beaten up.'

'But who deals with such matters?'

'The Customary Police.'

'And those who are persecuted can't go and complain?'

'If they did matters would be worse. The Wallisians know that well enough. Better pay the fine. As I've told you, we're living here in the Middle Ages.'

He got up, felt about in a drawer and came back with several sheets of roneoed paper.

'Here you are, this is quite recent. A sample of the stuff published by the Mission.'

He translated:

'Law concerning the Church. It is forbidden to avoid going to Mass . . . fine one dollar.'

'Why a dollar?'

'It's a hang-over from the time when the Americans had a

26

base on Wallis during the last war. There are no more dollars now and the fines must be paid in pigs or portions of a pig . . .'

'It is forbidden for men to miss Communion at Easter . . . fine one dollar. It is forbidden for women to come to Communion if wearing bodices with short sleeves, or made of muslin or low-necked . . . one dollar. Except in cases of absolute necessity, talking in church incurs a fine of two shillings. If anyone disobeys the beadle who orders him to remove, before entering the church, a piece of tobacco behind his ear or stuck in his earhole . . . fine two dollars. If anyone comes to church with painted hair . . . fine one shilling. If anyone is responsible for brawling in church . . . ten dollars.'

'Are there lots of laws like that?'

'Oh, that's only the beginning.'

'I want to take all that down on my typewriter.'

LAWS CONCERNING THEFT AND FRAUD

If a man gets an advance on the value of a pig he does not possess he shall pay a fine of . . . . 5 dollars

If a man kills a pig and eats it without telling the owner . . . . 10 dollars

If a man carries off an object in the belief that he owns it, he shall be pardoned the first time, but if he repeats the offence he shall pay . . . . 10 dollars

If an order emanating from the King or his Ministers is not carried out the culprit or culprits shall pay . . 5 dollars

If a man knocks a woman senseless in order to rape her, whether she is drunk and cannot defend herself or whether the man pretends he is her husband . . . . 22 dollars

LAWS CONCERNING TRAVELLING AND VOYAGING

It is forbidden for a man to walk at night in his own village . . . . 2 dollars

It is forbidden for the population of a village to go into another village for amusement. In the case of contravention a collective fine will be levied at the decision of the King or his ministers

It is forbidden to travel at one's own free will outside Wallis without royal permission

It is forbidden to pass in front of the King's *Kawa*

5 dollars

LAWS CONCERNING CONDUCT

It is forbidden to provoke anyone to fight.....5 dollars

It is forbidden to spread calumnies, or offensive remarks or to recall offences which have been forgotten

3 dollars

A woman may not go out unless wearing a bodice

3 dollars

It is forbidden to watch people bathing.......1 dollar

It is forbidden for men and women to bathe together

1 dollar

It is forbidden to expose oneself naked or to proffer obscenities................................10 dollars

Only the King or his Ministers may punish the faults of a married woman. If the husband himself punishes her

2 dollars

Illegitimate unions are forbidden...........22 dollars

If a man have sexual connection with a girl under the age of puberty............................20 dollars

Unfaithfulness of husbands or wives........22 dollars

If a man rapes a girl.....................20 dollars

If a man has connection with an ignorant or feeble-minded girl..............................15 dollars

If two men have unnatural sexual relations

20 dollars

If a man or a woman facilitates relations forbidden by law.......................................10 dollars

LAWS CONCERNING ANIMALS

If a man ties up his horse or bullock on the public highway.................................6 dollars

28

If a man rides on another man's horse without permission .... 5 dollars

If a man gallops his horse in a village .... 5 dollars

If a man frees a hobbled horse .... 5 dollars

If a man or woman allows a horse to mount a mare without the permission of the owner .... 5 dollars

If a dog bites anyone, the dog will be killed and the owner will pay .... 5 dollars

If the owner of a dog that has killed chickens or piglets refuses to put it down .... 5 dollars

If the owner of a pig refuses to pay for damage done by the animal, it shall be killed and eaten.

LAWS CONCERNING DEFERENCE

On the Royal Road to Mua, Hihifo, Lano and Mata Uru, the milk of the coconuts growing on the wayside may be drunk but not that of the nuts within the plantations .... 2 dollars

He who is alone must give way to a group of several persons. The crew of one canoe must give way to a group of canoes .... 8 dollars

Sick persons must not use washing or drinking water
2 dollars

It is forbidden for anyone with his hair whitened with lime to enter the King's property .... 3 dollars

It is forbidden to remain mounted on encountering the King, his Ministers or headmen on the public highway
5 dollars

Lack of deference to the King is forbidden .... 7 dollars

Lack of deference to Ministers or headmen is forbidden
5 dollars

Lack of deference to the French Resident is forbidden
3 dollars

I put all these sheets into a folder and marked it UKAZES. The little bungalow Benjamin Brial let to me was made of plaited bamboo panels and stood in a sort of miniature estate which stretched for about a hundred yards along the road that bordered the edge of the lagoon. Farther off, a wretched village of huts with palm-leaf, thatch or corrugated iron roofs straggled out along the shore and was half-hidden by very tall coco-palms. On the strand now uncovered by the tide, black pigs were rooting in the mud for the shell-fish that are their main food.

Towards Mata Utu the road came to an end in a wide square covered with short grass. There an astonishing spectacle awaited me. Facing the lagoon loomed the austere silhouette of a medieval cathedral. It had two square towers and its mere mass was imposing—formidable even—under the tropical sun. Looking rather like the supers in a Mystery Play, parishioners were standing about in groups near the canoes they had hauled up high and dry on the beach. It was not yet the hour of Mass. I felt I had been carried out of the stream of time, as though by some metaphysical mistake. I was witnessing the incredible link between the Polynesians, discovered only in the eighteenth century, and a monument of medieval faith which seemed to have been built in early Christian times.

The men were huge, their chests covered with sweaters ornamented with multi-coloured embroidery, and their *paräus* were caught at the waist by belts brightened with glass beads. On my earlier voyages I had been impressed by the Marquisans, most remarkable for their stature and strength. I could never forget a sailor at Nuku Hiva unloading from a schooner casks containing over forty gallons and handling them with no apparent effort. But that athlete, over six feet tall, and weighing at least a hundred and ninety pounds, would have seemed frail compared with the men of this group of Wallisians.

They were watching me out of the corners of their eyes. Despite their exceptional stature and majestic corpulence, some of the women in no way yielded to them as far as bulk was concerned, or in their noble bearing. Among a number I noticed the high, broad and rather bulging forehead which is characteristic of Malay women, and also the almond eyes. Solemnly, silently, more and more worshippers gathered round. They seemed to possess real, native charm and a sort of primitive power, but a power that was so to speak suppressed, tamed. And the general impression these people conveyed to you was one of the ineffable boredom one experiences in the face of passivity.

The next few days it rained. Rained as it does in Brittany, yet this was a tropical, equinoctial downpour of the worst sort, violent all the time but now and then aggravated by long drawn-out, deafening, thundering, hammer-blows, so powerful that one was seized with an unreasoning terror that they must precede an earthquake, a tidal wave. The sticky heat impregnated my belongings—my books and all the things already corroded with mildew.

I was weighed down with disgust and sluggishness. I felt myself falling to bits. The insistent buzzing of mosquitoes cut through the incessant drumming of rain on the palm-leaf roof of my hut. From its windows my view of Wallis was limited to a muddy beach lashed by a deluge. Everything beyond had vanished into an enveloping cloak of vapour. Women, like fleeing ghosts, hurried by on their way to the cathedral. Their black umbrellas sonorous in the rain, the bottoms of their velvet robes soaking wet and dragging in the pools and puddles of what had ceased to be a road, while their greasy, wavy hair hung dishevelled over their faces.

Then, quite suddenly, the sky cleared. The flaming sun appeared once more. Almost immediately the flowers, the palms, the thatches, the house-fronts were dry again. Pools disappeared and the mud road was hard once more. But the air was still insidiously damp, so that the least effort was painful. There was a dull but ever-present menace suspended over everything.

4 Opinions

I REALIZED that the existing situation was presenting a difficult political problem for the French administration, and I did not at all expect to be informed about its intentions by the Resident, to whom I went to pay a visit. This affable gentleman received me courteously but with necessary circumspection.

From the first I understood that a conversation about any other subject than the peculiar aspects of Wallisian folklore would hardly be tactful. We talked about the art of the *tapas*, which were still used for dance and ceremonial costumes, we discussed the 'tropical Douanier Rousseau' appearance of some of the compositions painted with vegetable dyes on broad strips of tanned wood-bark. I also learned that skin-diving gave only poor results, since the lagoon was relatively deficient in fish. The Wallisians practised collective fishing.

Any questions of another sort—although I was curious enough—would have been pure indiscretion. I did not know what the French Government proposed to do about the Wallisian royalty and the order of things it represented. I supposed that in their wisdom they wanted more or less the *status quo*, and thus the maintenance of this royalty which, with the passage of time, and the practice of democracy would become more and more representative. There remained that crushing majority of ninety-five per cent of the votes cast during the referendum.

Such a unanimity of opinion in favour of annexation to France and the adoption of its institutions, on the part of a people so obviously disciplined and obedient, constituted more than a revolution. What could the King think about it? What should I risk if I applied for an audience?

'dressed only in the traditional costume . . .'
'. . . and peppered point-blank by an army of tourists'

It was granted for the next day. I went to the palace with an interpreter, one Samino, a husky workman on Brial's staff. It is no doubt the most unpretentious palace in existence, to such an extent that we were held up for a long time by the problem of seating. The royal furniture in fact included only one chair and, as the King insisted that I also should be seated, one had to be borrowed from the Residency. During the wait we looked at one another in silence, smiling and embarrassed.

Finally, when all was in order, HM Tomasi *I* listened with apparent attention to Samino's speech introducing me as a Frenchman who had already done a trip round the world, on a sailing-boat of the same tonnage as that of Alain Gerbault (who was shipwrecked on Wallis), who sought for paradise in the Pacific Isles. Tomasi was a magnificent figure of a man, about forty years of age, dressed in a *paräu*, a European-cut jacket, a shirt and a tie—his best clothes.

He made no difficulty about answering my questions. He thought it necessary to maintain the Customary Laws (my 'Ukases') and thus the privileges of authority, as he judged them best to assure both the discipline and the happiness of his subjects. His reign would allow them to enjoy all the benefits of civilization. Wallis was going to get new roads, motor-boats, cars, radios, permanent building materials and other imports. A new hospital would permit of the wiping out of filariosis (a degeneration of the lymphatic system due to mosquito bites and causing elephantiasis), a task which was already occupying the French staff in the present hospital.

The King regarded President de Gaulle as a brother monarch from whom he expected generous help. 'The King he say very pleased General de Gaulle extend good helping hand to King of Wallis,' Samino translated. It was evident that the simple concept of democracy was quite incomprehensible to this smiling potentate. Despite all events, he regarded his régime as impregnable and his reign like the beneficent forces of nature allowing his people to take advantage of the benefits

'the Tourist Era'

offered by the annexation to France. I left the palace believing what I had up to then regarded as a joke: that Tomasi *I* himself had been the first to vote 'Yes' in the referendum!

What might be the opinion of the Bishop of Wallis? This frail old man with a long white beard had been on the island for fifty years. His kindly presence seemed almost unreal. He was noble, he was saintly. Maybe he had for long lived out of this world, in regions he would soon attain for ever. I could not see the slightest connection between the religious discipline that held six thousand Wallisian serfs as in a vice, and the beaming benevolence which emanated from the Bishop's eyes—still blue despite his years. I could not reproach myself with faintheartedness. I was confronted with a power which was based elsewhere than here on earth. Our conversation was an exchange of commonplaces.

5 *The Great Fishing of Ihifo*

BENJAMIN BRIAL jumped out of his old American truck, the only one on the island that still worked. I went over to him. He grabbed one of the huge, bamboo-handled harpoons leaning against the outhouse on the shore and aimed it at a piece of coral, which exploded to bits under the impact of the spear.

'If you'd like to come along tomorrow, I'll really show you something.'

His voice betrayed his excitement.

'What's going to happen?'

'A great fishing, with harpoons and canoes. I've just got back from Ihifo. For the last week everyone there has been getting ready for the right tide. Maybe there will be two hundred men and fifteen or twenty canoes on the reef.'

Would I like to go!

'We'll set out for Ihifo in the afternoon, and we'll sleep with the others on the little island over there on the other side of the lagoon. At sunrise everyone will be in his place, and then we'll start . . .'

The great double canoe slipped over the rose-pearl water. Far away, the first vessels of the long line ahead of us were already beached on the wooded islet where we were to spend the night. Disturbed in their domain the sea-eagles and frigate-birds glided up over the hillock where they had their nests, tiny black dots on the western sky.

When we beached in our turn, I could see that great preparations were going on. Not far from the water's edge the finishing touches were being put to a building about fifteen yards long and five wide, with its conical roof of palm-leaves supported by poles just cut from the neighbouring wood; it was a huge, fine-looking hut. On the slope of the coral strand holes had been dug and lined with slabs of madrepore, on which were laid edible roots, ears of maize and whole pigs whose agonized cries had only just died down. The food was covered with red-hot stones and on them were piled great bundles of blazing brush-wood.

The men's skill was as astonishing as their strength; one of them, who pulled up a tree by the roots as easily as we might pluck a handful of grass, also gracefully plaited a palm-leaf into a neat and elegant platter. My contribution to the feast consisted of some cans of corned beef and bottles of beer. I was astonished at first by the greedy excitement aroused by the opening of the cans, but I was even more amazed to see that my gigantic neighbours wrenched off the capsules of the bottles with their teeth!

Astonishment gave way to concern when they opened up the ovens containing the pigs. They had not had time to cook properly. Were they going to be eaten as they were? But as a matter of fact the meat was done to a turn—for Wallisian taste. So I had to do as they did, though I could hardly overcome my disgust at having to swallow raw flesh dripping with blood, and chew on a mass of tough fat which so hugely delighted my fellow-guests.

But what did it matter? The booming of the reef's waters, the glowing lights, the dark line of canoes hauled up on the beach, the glistening bodies of all the crouching men. I could imagine I was one of Wallis's crew feasting with the natives of an island discovered that very day.

This vision soon vanished. From far out at sea a black squall burst over the islet. No more stars. We crowded together under our shed. I said that perhaps the bad weather might last until the next day and that our fishing party might have to be called off, but no one agreed with me. One man began to sing.

His bass voice was soon accompanied by those of three old men near him. Before long the whole company was singing as a choir. It was a primitive, powerful song, a dialogue of Man with the Nature that he venerated, from whom he accepted everything, to whom he owed his existence.

The wind and rain slanted down, lashing the men's faces, but their grave, fervent expressions did not change. What did it matter if there was flood or drought? Was not everything the law of God, and had that law not allowed former generations to lead right up to our present lives? How can Man change things? And everything one cannot change is good. Squall followed squall all night long.

A great hubbub finally awakened me. It was daylight. The men were out on the beach, staring at the masses of heavy cloud scudding by and half-hiding the rosy glimmer in the east. I saw Benjamin in discussion with the leader of the fishing-party. What was going to happen?

Slowly the men formed into little groups by the canoes. Each man had his lance by his side, waiting for orders. Some of them had made a sort of visor out of palm-leaves fixed on their foreheads and fastened on the napes of their necks. All were obviously impatient, hard put to contain their eagerness. However, the daylight gradually grew stronger. It was very beautiful . . . the dull green of the lagoon against the barrier of dark clouds piling up as the tide imperceptibly drew out.

The various leaders suddenly separated, each one giving his own crew the long-awaited sign. The men rushed forward, and the canoes shot out together over the waters.

The flotilla of twenty canoes was deployed on a front of some one thousand yards, making for the broad coral pathway, now uncovered, which girdles the lagoon. Poles were plunged down in unison. The distance between the heavy craft shortened little by little, and soon the line was not more than five hundred yards long. Sometimes we crushed heads of coral that stuck out of water as pellucid as green crystal, in which we saw the first fish darting away. Then one of the leaders jumped waist-deep into the water and, except for two men in each canoe who kept it moving forwards, all the harpooners imitated him.

I leapt out too, and at once began to stumble on the crumbling coral. Though the delicate marine soil yielded under their weight, the men moved about with such agility that, despite all my efforts and the protection of thick rubber-soled boots, I was out-distanced. I kept tripping and getting scratched, while far ahead of me the first harpoons were flying out.

At last I felt the ground get firmer under my feet and I was walking on slabs of madrepore coral. The harpooners raised great splashing jets of water as they ran, shouting so loud that their cries cut through the monotonous, thudding boom of the breakers crashing on the other side of the reef. One old white-haired man, though afflicted with elephantiasis, ran like the others, on his monstrously swollen legs. How could they move about with bare feet on the jagged surface of the reef? The coral, the madrepore, were petrified into a surface made ragged by erosion and some of the excrescences must have been razor-sharp.

I lumbered along as best I could and joined up with a group following a school of blue carangues. There where the terrified fish were trying desperately to find a way out was nothing but a pool leading to narrow trickles of water and dry land. The fish piled up and were massacred by a hail of spears. One of them was impaled as it leapt into the air. An amber-coloured snapper, crazy with panic, tore open its belly on the rock and catapulted its massive head forward, only to be at once trans-fixed by a crunching iron blow. A harpooned globe-fish inflated itself instantly into an enormous white ball, bristling with prickles, and hurried off with its curious sculling motion.

The fish darted in all directions—anywhere, sometimes straight into the feet of the harpooners, who went on spearing

without letting up for a moment. It needed positively stupefy-
ing agility and skill to strike the spatulate-beaked snappers in
their course, so rapid were the movements of their black and
silver-striped bodies; or the young sharks zigzagging among
shoals of mullet; or the multi-coloured parrot-fish; or even the
slender, very long aiguillettes with huge beaks pointed as
swords.

A great sting-ray was surrounded. His flapping wings could
feel nothing now but dry madrepore coral. As he raised his
enormous tail and shot out the erectile prickles along its lower
part, he swung right round and prepared to rush forward . . .
three harpoons clashed in the middle of his body.

I felt a hand on my shoulder. A young lad pointed out to
me a spotted moray eel wriggling about a few yards off. The
youth stood stock-still an instant while he aimed, his leg and
left arm advanced, his hand flattened, his body bent backwards
on the flexed right leg. Then he hurled, and as he hurled he
went slack. The point of his spear nailed the slender black
head to the ground.

Every missile hit its mark. So unerring was their accuracy
that it seemed vaguely shocking.

It was no longer the case of a hunter aiming the arrow on
which his living depends; it was more a display of a sort of
miraculous automatism performing one of the essential acts
of survival.

The tide disclosed more and more of the reef. Up to now
the merous had remained motionless among the coral bushes
in whose branches they had been half-hidden, but now they
suddenly seemed to lose confidence in their protection. They
changed colour. They arched their broad, rounded tails and
dashed forward to seek some illusory shelter. As they were
brought to bay, in their fury they opened their bony gills and
armour-plated mouths, they raised their spiny manes and
looked as if they would leap upon the men. However, for the
fishermen it was child's play to strike them between and a little

above the two hollows on the head where the slightest thrust kills. They turn white as they die.

One of the fishermen ripped the skin off a surgeon-fish from head to tail with the point of his spear. Then he washed the flesh and ate it as it was. Another man scaled a mullet with his finger-nails and chewed it up bloody, living and struggling in his jaws.

A sudden brilliant flash of lightning was followed by the deafening roar and rumble of thunder right over our heads. The wind had dropped. Except for the brilliant white rollers that swept along and broke in silence, everything had become extraordinarily dark. Under the storm's flashes the lagoon's transparent fringe had assumed an unearthly hue. There was something unearthly also about that horde of men staring at the sky . . . like phantoms re-enacting the fishing of bygone times.

The old man squatted in front of his hut and dipped a little stick into one of husked half coconut shells containing dyes extracted from roots. He went on with his drawings on the *tapa* spread before him. The brown ochre formed first of all an irregular triangle, and then other geometric patterns. The world was so made, not by chance, but according to an order he was trying to represent. The old man took another little stick and dipped it into another shell. Then he surrounded his designs with broad, darker lines. Now he stopped and for a long time stared motionless at his work.

Not far from the old artist's hut a frangipani bush had scattered its fragrant blossoms and they stood out, ivory-white, against the green grass still damp from the last shower.

Under the low-reaching branches of trees the first canoe was just beaching.

'black pigs were rooting in the mud for the shell-fish that are their main food'

'and also their almond eyes'

overleaf: 'tapas, which are still used for dance and ceremonial costumes'

6 *Elections*

THE young and splendidly built postman jumped off his brakeless bicycle, let it fall to the ground, and held out to Benjamin Brial a little, square, blue, envelope—a telegram that he had pushed into the top of his *parāu*:

CHARTERED PLANE WILL BRING FRIDAY CANDIDATES SENATOR AND DEPUTY ELEC- TORAL CAMPAIGN STOP PREPARE LODGING FIFTEEN PERSONS.

So it was true after all. Wallis was going to have an election.

I hope M Loste, the present senator for Wallis, will forgive me if I say how extraordinary he appeared to me when I first saw him getting out of the DC 3 on the grassy runway. This company director, some sixty years of age, and a man of considerable distinction, was impeccably dressed in a navy blue suit with the rosette of the Legion of Honour in the buttonhole. His clothes were certainly cut in the rue de la Boëtie or in Savile Row. He had made just one concession to the climate. His hat was a fine pandanus straw ornamented with sea-shells. He removed this headgear and revealed his silvery locks as he saluted the numerous notabilities who had turned up to welcome him. Smiling and courteous, he at once began to shake hands all round. I realized all too well that it was I, dressed only in a *parāu*, who was really out of date.

M Loste, as well as his political opponents, stayed with Brial. M Loste's bungalow and mine were in fact close to each other, and I introduced myself to him. We got on together. He seemed to understand other people's point of view so well that I did not hesitate to say what I really thought. Without any transition, the Wallisians were going to be transferred

41

inside: 'controls that reduced human beings to the condition of serfs'
inside: 'painted with vegetable dye on broad strips of tanned wood-bark'
'the "tropical Douanier Rousseau" appearance of some of the compositions'

from a feudal régime of complete submission into a democratic régime of universal suffrage and freedom of vote. What would, what could, be the result? Would not politics run riot, would there not be excesses of all sorts? Was not Wallis an ideal theatre for the basest intrigues of rabble-rousers? I feared so.

'Quite frankly, do you think the Wallisians have much need of politics just yet?'

'Of course they've need of politics. First of all they must be represented. They can't go on living outside a world of which they are now officially a part.'

'How are they going to become a part of that world? Don't they run a risk of having their own world destroyed?'

'Destroyed? Destroy what? Do you realize the misery of these people? Do you know what is the standard of living of a Wallisian? Do you know that the average income is three thousand francs a year?'[1]

I had to admit that was not much. I thought to myself, however, that this sort of income had been good enough for the Wallisians to become the strongest and finest human specimens in the Pacific. No one denied that.

'So,' went on M Loste, 'what do they do? Well, they try to emigrate. There are two thousand of them working in New Caledonia now. There they get good pay in shops, factories and mines and they enjoy social security benefits.'

There came into my mind visions of a pit-head at Lens, of workers leaving a factory at Aubervilliers, of a workman's home a few days before wages are due.

'Oh, yes, I see all that, but what sort of happiness are they going to find?'

M Loste seemed astonished and looked at me closely.

'Happiness? What happiness? Where can it be found? Take a referendum on the other side of the world. What does a

---

(1) That is CFP francs, each of which equals 5.50 old French francs.

workman in the Renault works dream about? A Pacific island, the sun, a hut, living in a *parāu*, coco-palms, the lagoon, coral, fish. . . . And the Wallisian, who has all this permanently, what does he dream of? Why, to become a workman in a Renault factory.'

M Loste was right, what he said was absolutely true. My researches on Wallis were against the stream. M Loste had the right end of the stick. By anticipating their wishes this politician had become a living symbol of the life to which the Wallisians aspired. He was the representative of invincible progress. I could not fool myself. If I had been able by some impossible miracle to form a party on the spot, and had I attempted to woo the electors by publicly declaring my belief that 'Progress will bring with it evils greater still than those it overcomes', my electoral campaign would have finished in the lagoon. And they'd throw me out for preference where the biggest sharks were cruising about.

M Loste was opening the doors of a lovely new world. I would have been a reactionary more detestable still than those legists who drew up the 'Ukazes'. In fact my conclusion was that this was no place for me. I decided, just as though the choice had not been forced upon me, to take the first plane to Nouméa. I would work things out when I was there.

7 New Caledonia

No doubt it was Bougainville who first caught sight of the land which, had he landed, its natives would have told him was called 'Oajo'—that is, supposing that any communication other than by weapons could have been established between French sailors and cannibals who had never seen a white man. But the weather was bad, he was concerned about the health of his crew and he did not linger near the mountainous summits which appeared far off on the sea's horizon.

It was the famous Captain Cook who, on his second voyage round the world, discovered on 5 September 1774 an unknown island, on which he landed and which he baptized with the memorable words, 'It's a New Caledonia.' Indeed, the serrated ridges of high blue mountains, the plains and verdant meadows seemed to him another Scotland. Cook realized his discovery was probably important, but contrary winds and bad weather prevented him from much exploration. News of the discovery, however, reached the French Court, and Louis XVI entrusted Galaup de La Pérouse with a mission to go and reconnoitre these regions of the Pacific which might, perhaps, turn out to be a New World of unknown riches.

La Pérouse left Brest on 1 August 1785, but his ill-fated expedition never returned to France. What happened to his two ships, *La Boussole* and *L'Astrolabe*? In 1791 Bruni d'Entrecasteaux and Huon de Kermadec, in the frigates *La Recherche* and *L'Espérance*, were dispatched to find their predecessors. On the vast expanse of sea-routes they explored in vain. The years passed; despite the upheaval of the Revolution the French had not forgotten La Pérouse.

However, the second two navigators made a preliminary

survey of the greater part of New Caledonia. D'Entrecasteaux gave his name to the coral reefs which stretch out from the island to the north-east, and one of the islands which emerge from these reefs was to be called 'Huon'. Kermadec thought, maybe, that his Christian name was enough to give to a tongue of sand inhabited only by sea-birds and turtles—on the latter of which the crews feasted.

Thirty-five years later Dumont d'Urville, in another *Astrolabe*, found at Vanikoro (New Hebrides) proof that La Pérouse had been long dead and his frigates lost. From this unhappy voyage Dumont brought back—besides the tragic news—only the geographical position of the Loyalty Islands (to the north-east of New Caledonia) and a report on navigation in these waters rife with coral reefs. The first French settlement in New Caledonia was made by missionaries who, on 19 December 1843, landed from the frigate *Bucéphale*. Mgr Douarre and these Fathers of the Congregation of Mary (protected by an agreement the commander of *Bucéphale* had solemnly executed in the name of King Louis-Philippe with the principal chieftains of the coastal tribes) began a campaign of evangelization. But the King of France and his soldiers were very far off and the local sorcerers very near at hand. Soon the interpretation they and the native chiefs gave the 'treaty' forced the missionaries to relinquish their work. In constant danger of their lives, they had to retire to Kunie Island which they named the 'Isle of Pines'.

On 24 September 1853, Rear-Admiral Febvrier Despointes assumed possession, in the name of Napoleon III, both of New Caledonia and of the Isle of Pines. In 1854 Tardy de Montravel replaced the admiral and took up his quarters in the town of Port-de-France, the former Nouméa.

In the island were discovered mineral resources which rumour held to be practically inexhaustible. Was there not a chain of mountains extending several hundred miles? New Caledonia began to attract settlers and adventurers.

On 17 September 1940 New Caledonia joined the Free French, but on 12 March 1942, the 'Nickel Island' came into the war zone. The Japanese High Command was planning the invasion of New Caledonia, so the Americans brought planes on to the island aircraft-carrier and the troops destined for the terrible battles of the Pacific spent some time in New Caledonia. Every New Caledonian of about forty will shake his head and his face will cloud over when he hears the word Guadalcanal.

That, in a nutshell, is the story of this cigar-shaped island, about two hundred and fifty miles long, thirty-five across at its widest, set obliquely at the edge of the dangerous Coral Sea and at the western extremity of the Pacific. For anyone who wants to escape from Europe, the expression 'go to the ends of the earth' can be literally translated into geographical fact by a trip to New Caledonia, since the island is very exactly at the antipodes.

So I did not feel myself at all out of my element, at least during the forty-eight hours necessary to exhaust the attractions of this little, forgotten world. The attractions included a noisy, small, five-storeyed hotel, gaudy bi-coloured Cadillacs parked under the blossoming flamboyant trees in the *Place des Cocotiers*, which, believe it or not, were just taxis; and then there was the joy of reading month-old newspapers, eating raw fruit and vegetables, steaks and fried potatoes and Australian canned fruits, all of which were served at the restaurant opposite the cinema. And there, after the news-reel and a documentary on the Rocky Mountains, one could revel in a film entitled *Godzilla*.

Very soon the boredom of idleness in a small foreign town pressed heavily on me, and I reacted with some constructive thinking. There must surely be a thousand different things to do here. What might be the possibilities presented by this practically virgin country? I was beginning to dream of settling in some spot as yet undeveloped and of getting down

to do some development of my own—but an official handbook
proved sobering reading. I soon learned that,

'On an area of six thousand four hundred and fifty square
miles there are only twenty-one thousand inhabitants of
European origin (and of these more than one half live in the
one town of Nouméa) and twenty thousand Melanesians.[1]
The particularly favourable climate, the nature of the soil—
which is suitable for almost all crops—and the subsoil riches,
all combine to put New Caledonia into the class of economic-
ally favoured lands. However, the great distance from the
world's main markets and the proximity to territories which
are large-scale exporters of products identical with those of
New Caledonia, the lack of labour and of capital, have prevented the country from developing and progressing in a way
comparable with that of Australia or New Zealand.'

Fine. Just what is wanted to spur you on. But another piece
of literature informed me that,

'Nearly half the population of metropolitan French origin
has been settled on the island for several generations and,
naturally enough, this population not only has an assured
position in commerce but also owns the best land. One must
not be blind to the fact that settlement in New Caledonia
presents many difficulties to anyone who is not a skilled
manual worker or who is not possessed of a very considerable
amount of capital. The New Caledonian Chamber of Agri-
culture has many times warned intending settlers against
exaggerated optimism.'

So I decided to cruise about near New Caledonia. I knew
there was much beautiful scenery to be enjoyed. The most
sensible course to adopt—after I had made a good many
enquiries—seemed to be to hire a sound, fairly large coasting
vessel of, say, about one hundred tons. The price asked by the

---

(1) According to the latest census results this figure must be
increased by forty per cent.

captain of one such boat was not exorbitant—as it generally is, since piracy still flourishes among those who rent out ships and boats—and I agreed without haggling.

The very look of Captain Colliard made one want to put out to sea. His blue eyes and his smile beamed at the very thought; he was a well set-up, athletic man of about thirty with a tanned face and bursting with health. He would have made a good heavy-weight boxer and, indeed, something in his placid attitude rather indicated that he himself recognized this; however, he was first and foremost a sailor.

He was thoroughly French, but he looked like a direct descendant of the Vikings. With a passion for deep-sea fishing and a roving disposition, he had wandered to the ends of the earth. Recently he had been wandering between Australia and the New Hebrides, wherever there was fish and a market for it. He had just bought in Sydney the little vessel on whose deck we were chatting. He assured me she did not roll more than any other and that she behaved well at sea. To pass the time before he could get his boat fitted out for the next fishing season, he welcomed the suggestion of a little cruise towards the south and east. We could go first of all to the Isle of Pines and watch the fishing for giant turtles, then move up to the Loyalties where, with some luck, we might find whales that go there for the winter.

'The main thing,' he exclaimed, 'is not to get mouldy in port.'

His hawsers, made fast to the quay, crossed those of a grimy Japanese cargo-boat taking on nickel ore. We were deafened by the clashing of long iron girders which a liner's derricks were dumping a little farther off. Colliard would certainly be a good ship-mate. His boat was clean, neat, in good condition and ready to put to sea. We could get off in forty-eight hours.

'such treasures of originality should be preserved'
'so unerring was their accuracy that it seemed vaguely shocking'

8 The Isle of Pines

Narrator: In the paradise of Oro on the Island of Kunie there lived, long ago, two brothers. The elder was called Wamon and the younger Karoubéa. The two were such skilled musicians and they played constantly such ravishing tunes that the birds, the brothers' only neighbours, lived under a lasting charm, thinking that Oro must really be paradise on Earth. One day—though the Ancients were never able to tell why—the brothers made each for himself a flute out of green wood. They climbed the tallest mount of Oro and there, the one brother in the direction of the rising sun and the other brother in the direction of the setting sun, with their flutes gave forth their loveliest melodies. Karoubéa's flute, indeed, was as though enchanted. Never had such delightful music been heard. Little by little the birds gathered around him, as though bewitched. The skill and the success of his younger brother deeply wounded Wamon. He could not bring himself to admit his inferiority, especially before the birds. So, very early one morning, without even saying goodbye to Karoubéa, he left Oro. But Wamon's heart was broken, for he much loved his native region. He walked and walked for a long time, a very long time, and he crossed the Great Plateau and came to the lagoon's edge. But his hatred for his brother grew and grew, and still he was not far enough away. Finally he took the terrible decision to leave his beloved isle. By walking under the water he covered the distance between Kunie and the *Grande Terre.* But so great was his grief that he died and his ghost came back to Kunie to ask pardon of Karoubéa's ghost—for the younger brother was by now also dead. He vowed he would grow there the great columned pines[1] whose seed he had gathered on *Grande Terre*—and that is the explanation of why they are on Kunie.

An Elder of the tribe, arising: That is not true. It is not. It

---

(1) Araucaria, closely related to the familiar 'monkey puzzle tree'.

'the men rushed forward to the canoes'
'ahead of me the first harpoons were flying'

was Wamon who carried away the seeds of the araucarias from Kunie just before he crossed over to *Grande Terre*. When he walked on the east coast, each time he set down his foot a pine-tree sprang up. The araucarias there come from the Island of Kunie. On *Grande Terre* there was damn all.

THE great chief Barthélemy was clad in a '14-'18 uniform with the silk ribbons of First World War medals, now faded and frayed. He stood erect against a tall palisade of carved wood surrounding his hut. As he listened to me he had been chewing a bit of grass which he now pulled out from between his long teeth. He was well-built and tall: neither his body nor his face—with its shrewd expression—betrayed his sixty years.

'Maybe well men would like go to turtles,' he drawled. 'You are one of tourists who come now visit Isle of Pines?'

'No, not really. I travel and I write books.'

'Sort of journalist, eh? It's your boat moored since yesterday in Kuto Bay? Coming back from Vao on my horse I'm sure it was you I saw chatting with syndic.'[1]

I acquiesced.

'No lack of turtles all around the island on sand-banks. It's more difficult get a good team to go dive. There've been tourists here with photo, maybe cinema machines . . . Americans, Australians and fellows from I don't know where. They've given out too much cash. Now damned fishermen want lot of pressing. There was a time, oh yes, I'd only got to say word and if there was anyone objecting I gave him a good slash with my ray's tail and that was that. But nowadays the great chief is nothing more than damn all. Politics now, and all the whole bunch of parties and elections and I don't know what new things.

'I'm going to order them. I don't say it'll do good, that it'll work, but I'm going to try. We'll see. . . . Some of them

---

(1) The gendarme, who with the missionary is the only resident European, acts as registrar, civil engineer, postmaster etc: hence his name of 'syndic'.

looking after yams and taros, some practising football. And then we'll have to see if the boat's *ok*. But it's damned awful motor on that cutter, goes when it feels like, same as that man Joseph owns it. Maybe he say yes and maybe he say no. How much do you feel like giving them?'

I mentioned a figure.

The Great Chief nodded his head.

'Maybe the men, and that damn Joseph too, be glad to get little money. But I know what they want to be very happy.'

I knew too, the Isle of Pines men liked something even more than money.

'I've talked about that to the syndic and he's given me permission to take wine with us—not barrels and barrels of it but still enough for a little sea-trip.'

'Ah,' said the Great Chief.

For a moment or two he stared at me.

'Maybe you don't know what is the custom for the Great Chief?'

'Yes, I've been told about that—one or two bottles?'

'Whisky or rum, that's still better than the vino. And let's say two bottles instead of one, getting lonely all by itself.'

'That's all on board.'

'Well, well, I'll see, I'll try and arrange things; must come back here to Vao and I give you the answer.'

I shook hands with the Great Chief. As I smiled he straightened up to his full height, came smartly to attention like a stage trooper and favoured me with an ironical, burlesque salute by putting his long fore-finger to his greenish, moth-eaten forage-cap.

During the twenty hours' sail from Nouméa, in radiantly fine weather, we completely cut across the southern part of the great Caledonian Lagoon, dotted with coral-reefs, islands off which sperm whales were moving up north-eastwards in the direction of the Coral Sea. A strong ebb-tide made choppy water in the Nokanoui channel leading to Kuto Bay. We dropped anchor at the back of the bay on the sandy bottom of Kanumera bight. All around the boat, motionless at anchor, stretched the calm, unbroken lines of the deep bay; delicate but firmly outlined, emphasized for a long way by a curtain of filao foliage fringing the araucaria woods. An exposed coral reef smelling strongly of iodine bordered a rounded, rocky peninsula dotted with trees. A few birds. A great silence.

When we landed I clutched a handful of sand from the narrow strand. It trickled between my fingers, an almost impalpable ochre powder. Farther on shady paths between wild coffee-shrubs and century-old trees led up to stony slopes spangled with orchids, and then on to green hills.

The Isle of Pines owes its name to the thousands of araucarias that adorn its shores. Their dark, austere appearance, sweet and sad at the same time, is an harmonious contrast to the exuberance of tropical nature, tempering its garishness. The cypresses of Provence at the height of summer and in the silence of the day's heat, present something of the appearance and of the peculiar character of the Isle of Pines. There are places like human beings, unlike any other. Whoever glimpses this island will, in the first few minutes, be rewarded with a memory that will never leave him. It is an austral Eden.

Some four miles of picturesque track separate Kanumera bay from Vao, a village with a Catholic mission where live as a tribe most of the inhabitants of the island. The Kunie descend from a race of mercenary warriors and excellent sailors. In former days these born fighting men would set off in their large, decked canoes and settle by force of arms many a long drawn-out quarrel raging among the tribes of *Grande Terre*. The Kunie have remained famous for their skill and physical strength. They are passionately devoted to their native land and they hide under a sharp cunning (they have the sort of humour that would have pleased Bernard Shaw or, even more, Mark Twain) the fundamental hostility they feel toward all strangers. The Kunie men are smiling, at their ease and slightly sarcastic. Their manner implies that, while they tolerate foreigners, they owe them nothing but politeness. Nothing in the way one is treated ever induces one to think this subtle barrier of reserve could be overcome. A recent episode throws an interesting light on their attitude.

Jacques Soustelle, when on an official visit to the Pacific as a Minister attached to the person of the President, stopped at Kunie. When he had greeted the Great Chief Barthélemy and the principal notabilities, Soustelle was conducted to a group of huts shaded from the sun by splendid trees all hung with tricolour garlands. From the door of one of the huts emerged a native of about thirty, holding in his hands a thick sheaf of paper. The man was very decently clad in white trousers and a shirt with multicoloured floral designs, and he stood four-square on his big, bare feet. Without a word of introduction and with his eyes fixed on his first sheet, he began to address his illustrious visitor. All the tribe was gathered around in a circle.

'You, Jacques Soustelle, who since your earliest years have . . .' the firm, well modulated voice and its solemn accents caused the soldiers and civil servants composing the politician's suite to stiffen into an official pose. Soustelle's astonishment grew greater and greater as he heard a discourse that was at the same time a justification of his career and a detailed account of his life history. There was nothing that was not true, the chronology was faultless. This Melanesian with frizzy hair bleached by coral lime knew his life perfectly. Gaining in lyrical enthusiasm as he went on, he read sheet after sheet . . .

'You who devoted many years to the study of Aztec history, who, thanks to your erudition and assiduity . . .' and the heads of the attentive natives nodded in approval. Slowly the sun moved and its rays now cut through the foliage with full heat. The Minister, formally dressed with collar and tie, had to resign himself to hear recalled, with the date of each event, every detail of his career.

This is how it happened: the Kunie had been informed a long time ahead that an official visit was imminent, and they sent one of their number to gather information at Nouméa. And the man was not satisfied just with gleaning what the government or the Bureau of Native Affairs could tell him; he arranged for letters to be sent to Paris and various other places, so that he got back to the Isle of Pines with a mass of information about Jacques Soustelle which would have satisfied the most scrupulous Intelligence agent. (The Kunie all go to school and write very well, although they do transform French prose with their own poetic, flowery and noble style.) One of the men composed an ode. Perhaps his pen ran away into a certain grandiloquence, but certainly there was no statement which was not rigorously correct. The whole tribe could feel proud: from the address of welcome up to the *pilou*[1] of the Ghostly Fishermen which brought the great day to a close, it was plain that the Kunie knew how to do things in style. The Great Chief Barthélemy, assuming the carelessly ironic smile he kept for newcomers, was perfectly justified in saying to me after I had mentioned the story: 'Well, well, like that this fine fellow of a Minister was able to see that the natives of the Isle of Pines knew him better than he knew them.'

---

(1) The group dancing.

9 The Turtle Hunt

Rectangular, with palm-leaf roofs, walls and veranda of clay and coral lime, the Kunie huts are sometimes decorated with great shields of thick, dried leather—from the shells of the sea-turtles caught on the vast marine pastures which border the shores. Here the creatures come to graze on algae and grasses, crush the shells of the molluscs they eat, and stroll about in the shallow, tepid, luminous waters reflecting the rays of the sun. For the Kunie at all times turtles have formed an abundant supply of the best food offered by the ancient gods . . . an inexhaustible treasure of livestock.

RISING above the hills, the sun began to illuminate the little bay bordered with coco-palms and araucarias where the old native cutter rode at anchor. Ever since daybreak we had been watching from the shore the efforts of Joseph, the skipper, to get his motor working. He straightened up and hauled himself out of the open cockpit. His face was contorted with rage and running with sweat.

'You don't talk to your engine,' said Barthélemy, as he stuck the bit of grass he had been chewing between his teeth. 'You angry with each other?'

The dozen men in *paräus* who were squatting on the sand roared with laughter. Joseph grabbed an enormous, rusty adjustable spanner and threatened the engine with it. He was so furious that I thought he was going to smash the motor to pieces, but he merely directed at it the most abominable volley of curses I had ever heard in my life.

'Oh, oh, mustn't give it hell like that,' shouted Barthélemy. 'Must talk to it nicely . . . maybe you think you're talking to your *popinée*?[1] Now it's going to really get angry. You've no respect for old age, Joseph. That's not right.'

The laughter broke out anew, louder than ever.

'They told you clearly not to shove that motor in boat that had been sunk for more than thirty years. Maybe it's a bit rusted after all that time,' put in one of Barthélemy's sons—one-eyed and very fat.

'That bad Joseph, he sold the petrol to buy beer and he filled up his tank with sea-water,' another mocked.

'He's used the oil to fry his yams.'

All that did not console us for having missed a turtle hunt. It was becoming more and more probable that I would soon get back to Colliard, who had been kept on his boat by some unexpected and urgent job of work. Joseph, however, had now once more gone down into the cockpit. We could hear him cursing the ancient piece of machinery. He was handling it very roughly indeed. His voice emerged from the cockpit, accentuated by the thumping and crashing of tools, raised or lowered with every variety of intonation from persuasion to command, from supplication to the most violent anger. At last, just as I had decided to wait no longer, there came the miraculous tapping—soon lost in the cheers of my neighbours—that announced the engine's restoration to life. But could we dare to hope such a miracle would last?

'All right, let's go,' shouted Joseph, sweeping the sweat from his forehead with his forearm. 'That bloody motor, once it's started you can't stop it.'

The sea-turtle is an amphibious creature. By eking out the air in his lungs as parsimoniously as a hibernating mammal, he can remain for a very long time motionless on the sea-bed, using the undulations of the ground to hide or cover himself. When he cruises about, during which time he wisely husbands his strength, he surfaces at regular intervals and slowly and

---

(1) Wife.

'the most lovely beach I had ever seen. Its perfect curve stretched for several miles round the inside of the atoll'
overleaf: 'about a hundred children . . . hurling up sand as high as they could'

thoroughly replenishes himself with oxygen before once more continuing well below the surface. If he is alarmed, he is capable of making off with strong, rapid strokes, but after the first spurt his speed is reduced and he has difficulty in repeating such efforts unless the air in his lungs is renewed.

If he is tenaciously pursued, he soon begins to suffocate. As he has to take this indispensable air while constantly threatened and harried, panic forces him to keep up a speed that tries his strength to the utmost. This is the way the Kunie hunt the turtle. In fact their method is that of a marine fox-hunt.

No doubt we should have all been pitched into the water if the motor had stalled when the cutter got into the tumultuous breakers of the narrow channel. However, the engine went on working splendidly. But the little boat was dreadfully rocked and shaken before reaching the calm, shallow waters over the sandy bottom dotted with star-fish which forms a broad plateau bordering the shore.

A lively lad of about fifteen had not had time to climb the mast before he yelled, 'Turtle!' The men all moved forward.

'Where? Where?' I shouted.

'Look, right ahead,' answered the look-out boy. 'And he's diving.'

I was just in time to see, fifty yards or so away, a big, brown shape dive down in an eddy.

'A small head,' Barthélemy said contemptuously as he leaned against the mast. 'He don't weigh more than fifty pounds.'

A man had perched himself on the overhanging part of the bows, holding on to the stay with his left hand. With his right he was signalling to the man at the wheel and indicating the changes of direction in the turtle's flight—even the creature's apparent intentions, as he saw them. I could now make out quite distinctly the turtle swimming along the sea-bed.

Aft, the man at the wheel concentrated on making our little boat follow the changes of course that fear or cunning sug-

'the fruits of the Garden of Eden'

gested to the hunted turtle. From a plane the boat would have looked like some drunken body spinning in arabesques. I was fascinated by that brown hand up forward. It seemed animated by a double life; it was both a mobile signal and an instrument that in some way possessed the power to destroy the creature struggling down in the sea's green transparency.

Obliquely the turtle surfaced. The men shouted, and their shouts became savage roars as the yellowish head appeared. His beak open, breathing greedily, he turned and telescoped toward the boat that bore down upon him. Twenty yards, fifteen, ten. I could make out his glaucous eye, seemingly covered with a whitish haze.

Suddenly the creature plummeted. In a few moments he had gained maybe thirty yards on us. The guiding hand motioned to bear to starboard . . . more . . . more. Always to starboard. Then it remained flat while we steered straight towards the shore. Then suddenly the hand motion to steer to port . . . to port . . . right round. We were soon gaining on the turtle, at times so near that a harpoon could certainly have struck it. Clearly also the creature was now in distress. The flippers' broad strokes were slowing, sometimes scratching the sand. His fatigue was more and more obvious. Suddenly he slowed and came up for air, neck at right angles to body, like a man freed from a stone holding him to the sea-bed. He staked everything on a last throw. He was breathing spasmodically, in great gulps.

The boat was right on top of him. Two men jumped overboard and disappeared in their own spray. I had not even time to snatch my submarine mask before they were up again, each holding one of the creature's flippers and with the palms of their hands at the base of the shell, keeping the turtle upright. Out went a rope: it was knotted and the prize hauled on board. Barthélemy had been right. All the men agreed the weight was from forty-five to fifty pounds. The head appeared curiously small compared with the amber brilliance of the beautifully marked shell. The turtle was turned on his back and put down in the hold.

'Now, maybe we'd better get down to real business,' said Barthélemy. 'The Great Chief first of all! . . .' and he held out his cup to the lad who was pulling the cork from the demijohn of wine.

After a third 'small head' had been dropped down in the hold, Barthélemy thundered, 'But, God almighty, what's these damn-all turtles we're catching nowadays?'

He bawled out to the men forward:

'I don't want to see such rubbish aboard. What you're bringing up is just mosquitoes!'

He raised his cup and held it out. 'Gives me a bellyache to see this sort of thing. Must have swig of vino to cure it.'

But the size of turtle we ran across some minutes later shook even Barthélemy from his indifference. Not only did he now share in the excitement which gripped the crew, but in fact became the keenest of them, and took personal command of operations. He was no longer a sarcastic old man philosophically accepting his duty to maintain his traditional dignity: he was the Great Chief in action, the man who had judged offences against Custom and had administered punishment with strokes from a ray's tail.

Now he had forgotten his French. With the air of authority and power before which everyone had formerly bowed, he shouted his orders in Kunie. No one now paid the slightest attention to my presence. No one answered my questions. Nevertheless, I got the distinct impression that Barthélemy was taking up something that had been interrupted a long time before; that he had a personal score to settle with the enormous creature, which everyone appeared to feel it was of the highest importance to capture.

The turtle had dived and was unhesitatingly headed in a direction that provoked lively alarm on board. The motor was pushed to the limit. It made an infernal din—but no one worried about that. When I recognized we were near the narrow passage we had come through earlier, I realized what the turtle meant to do. The sandy plateau would soon give way to a slope where a blue line marked the frontier of the sea's depths. If the great chelonian managed to reach them, he was saved. It was a game of chess between him and Barthélemy in which the former staked his life and the latter his reputation.

A first ruse nearly left victory with the turtle. A jumble of dead coral branches covered the bottom of a great, brownish expanse; into this the turtle slipped. At one moment he was swimming along, at the next he had vanished. Disappeared, invisible. He was certainly hiding there where he was the best disguised, but where? The men stared and stared in vain. The boat turned round several times above the spot where the turtle seemed to be, but with no other result than to arouse the fury of Barthélemy, who hurled curses at a crew as baffled as himself. One diver jumped overboard. He swam several times, and for minutes at a time, under water and seemed more and more vexed each time he surfaced. His eyes, though well enough trained, could not make out the whereabouts of the great turtle's shell. Another man jumped.

Barthélemy let out an inarticulate cry. By a lucky chance the man had flushed the creature and it almost jostled him as it made off. No question of losing a moment in picking up the divers (who were, indeed, already making for the shore, although it was a good way off). In any case the turtle had gained and was maintaining a considerable lead. But he lost much of it as he drew near the channel, and this Barthélemy, who was manoeuvring marvellously well, had foreseen. The turtle's next trick, however, took both crew and chief entirely by surprise. He popped up like a cork and faced the boat— seemed to wait for it, while at the same time breathing like an automatic pump. Fifty, thirty, twenty yards . . . ten . . . the men were going to jump. The turtle bent forwards, and plunged *towards* the boat, and passed under it. Before the boat had slewed round completely and had headed in his pursuit, the turtle had turned again and was far away, dashing toward the channel.

Then he made a mistake. He surfaced and noted what a good lead he enjoyed, and he plunged *without breathing*. From the deck then he was invisible, nor could his real direction be judged. The boat just went forward blindly. It seemed a long time before Barthélemy's sullen look gave way to an outburst of joy. The turtle's yellow head had just emerged again. From its position on the water even I could see he was exhausted. We gained on him rapidly even after he had set off once more. The channel was still a good way off. This was the finish.

He was soon swimming just below the surface not more than a cable's length ahead; then half a length only. A semi-circular bit of cartilage was missing from one of his hind flippers. Had a shark nicked him? I could count the parasites sticking on the huge carapace. I could not believe that the two young men preparing to jump would be able to grab hold of such a monster. They leaned forward, attentively watching the last phases of the turtle's exhaustion.

I slipped on my rubber fins and my diving mask. The water was not more than twelve or fifteen feet deep. Barthélemy's orders rang out as the divers sprang off. I imitated them a few moments later. When my field of vision was cleared of bubbles I could make out the turtle scurrying along on the sea-bed. The two men were just going to seize him. How did they manage to find their way so surely without fins or goggles? The first man grabbed the turtle's hind flippers and was dragged along a little, but did not let go. He was soon helped by the second man. Their weight behind acted as a counter-weight, while the creature used its free fore-flippers to paddle away furiously. The inevitable result was that the turtle was soon swimming perpendicularly, headed for the surface—above which presently he appeared. Then the lads swiftly and adroitly let go of the hind-flippers and grabbed hold of the fore-flippers. His fore-limbs now were paralysed and the thrashing of the others kept upright the huge three hundred pound mass. This astounding capture was not due to the men's strength—that would not have sufficed—but to the turtle's own power. The ancient Japanese would have understood and highly appreciated this transposition of judo principles— the utilization of an adversary's strength. All the same, the turtle had to be kept on the water. He tended to slip back once more into a horizontal position but was prevented by the men's bodies flattened against his, pushing in opposite directions.

Abruptly, the neck stretched backwards and the wide-open beak attempted to bite. If these sharp, gigantic pincers had snapped the men's arms or shoulders they would have been cut right through. But the lads kept a sharp watch and roared with laughter at the vain efforts of that terrible head. However, men and turtle were beginning to sink and it was by now high time to throw out a line.

It took a lot of effort to haul the creature on board and turn it over on deck. This turtle was indeed an old friend of Barthélemy's. He was recognizable not only by his size and by the nick some shark had bitten out of one of the flippers, but by the deep scratch a harpoon had at some time scored on the carapace. Furthermore, Barthélemy himself had missed this gigantic turtle on two previous occasions.

'So, you old fathead, you thought you'd like to shoot off again, eh? Maybe you're bigger and fatter now than last time we spotted you. While you were around enjoying yourself, you know what you were doing? Well, you were making some nice, tasty meat for us!'

As a joke Barthélemy put a harpoon shaft close to the turtle's head; in a flash the beak crunched on the wood and shattered it to splinters. The divers, still snorting and blowing, burst out laughing.

'Say, Great Chief,' teased Joseph, 'maybe we'll have to see about getting a pension if a little fellow like that messes up one of the Kunie fishermen! Must ask about that when the next *zozo*[1] comes along to talk politics to the tribe. That would be something quite different from the little gunshot and damn-all shell-splinters you picked up while you were enjoying that round-trip to France.'

Barthélemy beamed with delight. Nothing pleased him more than to hear references to his having been wounded in the '14-'18 war. He held out his mug and knocked it against the step of the mast.

'Well, well, that's all right in its way, but you're forgetting something . . .' and he pointed to the demijohn already three-quarters empty.

Later in the day, after a seventh turtle was down in the hold now smelling strongly of musk, Barthélemy said:

'I think it's all right like that, what? Mustn't do like those damned Americans a hundred years ago, maybe less than that. The country was full of wild animals enough to give good meat to everyone . . . well, there was damn-all left when they'd done in all those bisons, or cows or bulls or whatever they were, on the prairies. . . . Buffalo Bill's gang and all that . . .'

For the last time he held out his mug but the boy, his hair bleached with coral lime, held the demijohn upside down between his arms and wagged his head to Barthélemy. Nothing doing.

'What are we going to do? Plan our route?' asked Colliard to me one morning as the kettle was humming on the portable stove. 'We'll soon have seen everything that's to be seen here. The weather looks as though it'll keep fine and there must be swarms of whales at the Loyalties.'

I could not help laughing. Colliard was trying to tempt

---

(1) That is 'European', from the New Hebrides word '*Manzoreille*'.

me. He got bored to death in port. Maybe there is a sort of interpenetration between the two—a man and the ship he commands. A boat that is built to sail makes rather a pitiful object when she is tied up. A real sailor cannot long remain deaf to the words, 'Let's go.'

And I was secretly satisfied. I was being invited to move on, and that was splendid. After all, the taste for wandering, that malady, that itch of curiosity were not peculiar to me. I could always find others to whom I could make the same reproach: *Terrible, terrible this inability to settle down, where will it lead me to?*

Moreover, Colliard was right, we had seen almost everything here. It is first glimpses that really count . . . the stalactite and stalagmite grottoes remind me of the *Voyage en Chine* of Bibi Fricotin or some other hero of the coloured magazines of my childhood; the cells of the Commune prison in rows like a concentration camp, now overgrown with bush and used as a chicken-run (*and to think that political prisoners were shut up here and even a woman Louise Michel!*); eroded rocks like thousand-ton tops, or like meteors stuck in Gadji Bay. But there were no whales hereabouts; they could be seen only far away off the island, a hundred Moby Dicks—though they were not white and we still had our two legs.

'HM Tomasi *I* . . . dressed in a *parāu*, a European-cut jacket, a shirt and a tie—his best clothes'
'"the Wallisian, what does he dream of? Why, to become a work-man in a Renault factory"'

10 *Lifou*

Garçons de Lifou, qui fumez la zindgarette,
Le tabac, c'est du m'poison
La fumée, ça fait tourner la tête
Et ça me fait perdre la raison.

Lifou boys who smoke cigarettes,
  Tobacco, it's my poison
Smoke it makes you giddy
  And makes me lose my wits.

(From a song.)

ABOUT thirty miles from the Isle of Pines we sighted our first whales, all heading on the same route north towards the Loyalty Islands. And now, anchored off Lifou, we could see a good dozen of the creatures.

Colliard had warned me before we made our landfall but still I could not get over my astonishment at a strange freak of nature: the western extremity of Chepenée Bay is carved into the *exact* shape of a whale and it overlooks the real whales playing below. There are always some of these huge animals that pass the winter in this immense indentation. From a few miles, with the use of a little imagination, the likeness appeared all the more striking, since araucarias grow where the blow-holes would be, looking like spurts of water.

We were comfortably anchored in deep water. It seemed prudent to stay as far away as possible from a sheer coast that offered no shelter and where, as Colliard aptly remarked, nothing would be easier, when the wind was blowing from the west, than for a 100-ton vessel to be smashed like a matchbox on to the rocks.

'the fruits of the Garden of Eden'

'My God,' he added, his eyes dancing. 'Do you realize what sport it would be if we were allowed to hunt those sardines?' Followed by her calf, there was a whale as long as our boat cruising about lazily not a hundred yards from us. Another was floating at a stone's throw from the shore. Two others were smacking the surface with the flat of their white tails and shooting up jets of water several yards high with a noise like the discharge of big guns. Maybe they were mating?

We were accustomed to associate whales with arctic solitudes and this association of ideas did not seem inappropriate in the landscape around us. Its harshness was accentuated by the grey, cloudy weather. I have never seen anything more austere in all the tropics than this very tall island, with sombre cliffs falling abruptly into the ocean depths. Here is the greatest gathering of cetaceans visiting this part of the Pacific, and it remains during each austral winter—that is to say, from July to September, or mid-October sometimes. Years ago, whaling was carried on very actively in these parts, but it has been forbidden for the last seventy years. The legends of Lifou comprise a number of stories brought back by sailors who served in British or Australian whalers. However, at present, for the six thousand or so Melanesians who live on the huge block of limestone that is their island, the seasonal arrival of the largest animals in creation serves for little else than to announce that the time has come for looking after the yam fields.

A copra shed, the buildings of the Protestant Mission, the ruins of a Protestant church, some huts . . . not a vessel near the chalky rocks—there is nothing much to encourage exploration, and I spent the remainder of the day watching the movements of the whales. They were no doubt animals of the *Megaptera* sort (humpbacked whales), though I would not swear all were of the same kind. The *Megaptera* whales are described as not exceeding about sixty feet, except very rarely, whereas the largest of the whales, the blue whale, reaches

eighty-five feet and maybe even more. The colour of the beasts
I watched through my glasses was a blackish grey, occasionally
rather bluish, and certainly some of them were more than
sixty feet long. The calves, whose skin was considerably
lighter in colour than that of the full-grown animals, ranged in
length from about fifteen to twenty-five feet. They kept
playing around their mothers, or rather against them, for the
young ones never left their parents' side, despite their lively
jumps and capers. And though the calves comported themselves crazily enough, they seemed fully conscious of the
gigantic placid masses protecting them from danger. Such
dangers might well be very real ones. An old fisherman
I talked to said he could not remember ever having seen
grampus in these waters—that is, the 'killer whales', which,
since he had sailed the seven seas for more than twenty years,
he could have recognized readily enough—but he showed me
a long miner's bar which had been forged into a harpoon
and which he had not straightened up again after it had
been bent at right-angles. This was a souvenir—and a proof—
of a combat he had waged against a twenty-five foot shark
he met prowling along the shore. It was so heavy it had been
impossible to haul it completely out of the water.

How fickle is our nature; how doggedly boredom waits
for those greedy for impressions, if we do not renew them.
Commonplace enough observation, I know, but by next
morning the whales had become commonplace. They had
nothing more to offer me.

Colliard shared my feelings. 'They're so big you can't do
anything but look at them, and once you've observed them
carefully and reflected how small we are compared with them,
well we're not going to stop here a month of Sundays.' As a
matter of fact, Colliard spent most of his time with a rod
angling for the surgeon-fish which moved in shoals under
our boat.

I was more interested in the preparations being made by about a dozen women in 'Mission' dresses on an irregular bit of level ground not far from the shore. Through my glasses I could see one of them was hammering with a mallet and driving small stakes into the ground. Others were throwing balls at each other. 'I've got it,' shouted Colliard in reply to my question. 'It's Saturday. The women are going to play their cricket match. We mustn't miss that.'

The crews of the British whalers of long ago had not only left behind them the normal legacies—their religion, their venereal diseases and their cricket—but also undoubted evidence of fraternization, as witness the blue eyes, the fair hair and the light complexions which lent some of the women an excitingly attractive appearance. One young girl, graceful and slim in her green muslin flowing robe, her bluish-green eyes sparkling in a honey-coloured face, seemed to me the most ravishing I had ever met. Colliard, was was squatting next to me among the audience, made a significant grimace and wagged a warning forefinger. He whispered in my ear, 'Finished. The good old days of the whalers are finished. We were sized up well before we landed from the dinghy. Not a ghost of a chance here for old devils like you.'

Even if I had to watch a hundred cricket matches I am afraid I would not get the hang of the rules, but that did not matter at all. Our row of spectators was propped against a low wall of fossil madrepore coral, whose beautiful convolutions I had admired before sitting down (such material would make the most beautiful and original houses). The match took place facing the sea and the movements of the players—all in ample, multi-coloured Mission robes—somewhat masked the movements of the whales (which were so close in shore that for a moment I thought one of them was stranded). The cries of the women slanging one of the team, the shouts of encouragement or of vexation from the crowd, the whistles, the banging of spoons on a tin or an oil-drum, all this cacophony accompanied the ups and downs of the game, while from the sea came continuously the tremendous banging of the whales' tails on the water's surface. If a European child had been put among us, it would have said afterwards, 'The whales came to watch the match and they clapped with their tails for applause.'

'By the way, have you noticed the weather?' said Colliard to me when everyone had cleared off except us and a few children. 'I'd like to go aboard and take a look at the barometer.'

Decidedly it had dropped a good deal. Colliard was right not to risk having to put up with bad weather at so uncertain an anchorage. We would sail round the island westwards and once we were out of the bay we could decide what to do according to the state of the sea. I shared Colliard's keen dislike of the idea of beating about at night in front of a boat-trap. We soon discovered that the wind, which by now was quite fresh, was very definitely not favourable to us. The distance we could make before nightfall would clearly not take us to Gaatsha. So we decided to make for the east coast of New Caledonia, towards which anyway both wind and wave seemed likely to carry us.

A few hours later the wind shifted.

Few waters in the whole vast Pacific have a worse reputation than the channel between the archipelago of the Loyalty Islands and New Caledonia to the west. In normal weather, the sea there is choppy, ill-tempered, unreliable—in fact a sort of tropical English Channel. In heavy weather navigation is practically impossible. Very few vessels take this route, tragically celebrated for the number of its shipwrecks.

As we had a head wind, the weather got worse and worse. In four hours we did not cover ten miles. The heavy coasting vessel strained and groaned in the seething waves and her solid ribs shuddered under the vain throbbing of the motor. As dawn broke we were still making no headway. Spray dashing against the windows rendered visibility nil. Colliard at the wheel stared with bloodshot eyes, red from sleeplessness, and sometimes could glimpse the prow of his vessel plunging into a sea the colour of slate. Anxiety deepened the wrinkles on his broad, crumpled forehead.

Suddenly, a wave carried the boat high up and let her fall with such violence that, despite her stout build, I was afraid for a moment she would split in half.

'No. We can't go on,' yelled Colliard from the poop-deck. 'It's impossible.'

I looked at the raging sea.

'What are we going to do?'

But I was facing the wind on deck and my voice did not carry.

He pushed his head and shoulders out and a spurt of spray lashed his face.

'What? What are you saying?'

I bawled through the funnel of my hands: 'What are we going to do?'

'We've got to stop sailing in this bloody channel. Even beating about we've no chance of reaching the east coast for God knows how long. There's sure to be a tremendous sea near the reefs. What we really ought to do is to make for Nouméa, but that's a hell of a way . . . the best thing is to take shelter at Ouvéa and to wait there for the weather to calm down.'

Colliard was right and all I could do was to agree. He swung the wheel with all his strength and we headed for the great atoll of Ouvéa, away toward the north-west where the wind was carrying us.

Under a sky of rushing, dark and enormous clouds, we at last made out the breakers and then the seething entrance to the sea-passage into which we rode. The sea was foaming at the foot of low cliffs edged with coco-palms that bent and bowed under the fury of the tempest. The waves carried us on. We entered the comparative peace of the lagoon and cast anchor on a sandy bottom in about five fathoms of water, well protected by the curve of the beach about two hundred yards away. The chain stopped rattling in the hawse-hole and the motor died away. It was only then I realized the full force of the wind. The blasts tore along at more than sixty miles an hour. The barometer was dropping rapidly. Not far from our refuge, the surroundings of the passage were just a wild, heaving mass of livid white. The sky grew darker and darker, the torrential rain blotting out the coast entirely. I went down to shelter in my cabin; no sooner had I flopped on to my damp bunk, than I fell into a stuporous sleep.

All that day and all the next night the tempest raged. We rolled a lot, for little by little the lagoon's waters got choppy. The morning weather bulletin from Radio Nouméa announced that a tropical depression coming from the Banks had reached the Loyalties and New Caledonia: at times the wind had been more than fifty knots and flooding and much damage had been reported at several points on the eastern side of the *Grande Terre*.

Colliard made a sour face at me.

'So we're not so badly off here. If we'd gone on we'd have been in for one hell of a time.'

I could imagine what it must be like out at sea: we'd had a narrow escape. Still, we were not completely happy where we were. It was getting more and more difficult to stand upright. I scalded myself with the teapot at breakfast and when I had swallowed what was left of the tea I was overcome by seasickness. Nothing is worse than to be at anchor and still have to sway and rock in a heavy swell. I went on deck. The sharp, fresh air brought me round. Everything was grey and sullen. Waves were breaking very high on the immense, deserted beach. A seagull was swept along by the wind with a shrill cry. I shuddered, went below again and shut myself up in my cabin.

Thus we remained for fifty hours, only keeping watch to see that our moorings were all right and to examine the barometer, which was obstinately stuck at TEMPEST. I felt seasick all the time. Then, almost abruptly, the weather became radiantly fine, although the wind was still far too strong for us to set out to sea. Under the sunlight the lines of the nearby coast stood out with startling clearness. The leaves of the coco-palms glistened and sparkled. I felt all at once such an urge to go and stretch my legs that I would have jumped into the sea to get to the beach, if Colliard had not agreed, despite the difficulty, to launch the dinghy. I did not have to row. A huge, long wave, towering above me, rolled up and picked me away from the side of the boat. The translucid curve of the breaker swelled out, then hollowed, and as it unfurled itself, I was carried so high up on the beach that the bow of the little boat was thumped down with a great crash just on the edge of the dry sand. I pushed the dinghy on a little and then jumped out.

I was thrilled with delight, the delight that all sailors know so well after they have been long exposed to the sea. At first step, the first look round, and I was convinced I was walking on the coral strand of the most lovely beach I had ever seen. Its perfect curve stretched for several miles around the inside of the atoll: it widened near the passage before it died away on the threshold of a vast curtain of greenery. I went on across the width of the beach. What had seemed from the boat to be quite deserted was in fact a grove of coco-palms sheltering a charming village. As a precaution against the cyclone, all the boats had been hauled up high and were out of sight under palm-thatch sheds. Men wearing *paräus*, women in dresses of bright colours, naked children came forward to meet me.

A few hours later I got back to the boat. It was still dancing about in the swell.

'Colliard, old man, I'm stopping off here.'

'the Word'
overleaf: 'this apparently effortless masterpiece—my palace of palms'

'What?' His face expressed complete stupefaction. 'Here?'

'Yes, here.'

'But you're nuts. What's happened to you? What do you think you'll find here?'

'Oh, I'm not hoping to find anything any more. I've found it. In fact, I think I'd be nuts if I *didn't* stop off here.'

'But there's nothing here at all. You must think it over.'

'As far as I'm concerned there's everything. Too bad for me if I'm wrong. I'll take the consequences.'

'But we've got on all right, haven't we. There's nothing wrong there, is there?'

'No, no, of course not. Quite the opposite.'

I picked up my baggage, paid the still stupefied Colliard what I owed him, including the return run to Nouméa, shook him heartily by the hand and got off the boat.

To tell the truth, I had fallen in love at first sight with a practically unknown place. Maybe I had done something foolish. I was not even at all certain the natives would accept me and put me up. I had spoken only to a few men: it was true they were obviously men of importance, and they had treated me with kindness and seemed to like me, but they had also informed me that it would be necessary for me to present myself to the chief of the tribe I wanted to stay with. A young man had already been sent off on a half-wild horse to find the chief on the other side of the island—the side facing the open sea—where he was inspecting his herd of goats.

Now that I was about to land on the beach for the second time I was apprehensive. According to Melanesian custom I had prepared a present as a mark of respect for the chief. But had I not taken too much for granted his favourable reply to a request that I had not yet made? These thoughts were chased from my mind by shrill cries coming from the village— about a hundred children were rushing to meet me. They were shouting with joy and throwing handfuls of sand high up into the air. When they got to where I was, they stopped and

inside: 'this apparently effortless masterpiece—my palace of palms'
'wives from among the black-skinned natives'
'the imperturbable Benoît'

closed in, but went on hurling up sand as high as they could. The spray rose in ochre spurts against the vivid blue sky and then fell in arches, like fountains playing powder. The children's wavy hair was covered with this dust, so that they seemed to be wearing eighteenth-century wigs.

I was dazed by all these cries and movements. The sand got into my eyes and my mouth, but I managed to walk on and to make myself heard. A child of about five or six was pushed forward. His waist was girt about with a bit of a faded *paräu*. He was the most charming child you could imagine. I found out eventually that he was the son of the chief. An expression of marvellous surprise spread over his face as he looked up at me. I asked him his name, and a hundred shouts answered, 'Iviki Atule, Iviki Atule': that means 'little mackerel'—the most lively fish. I took Iviki Atule's small brown hand and he led me to his father's hut.

Pierre Dumai, the chief of the tribe of Mouli, accepted my presents and shook me by the hand. He was a man of about forty; slim, of medium height, well-proportioned, and his vigorous lithe body seemed to express his self-assurance and habit of command. His face showed liveliness and intelligence, while its agreeable features and his light skin clearly indicated a Polynesian origin. He expressed himself in excellent French, with scarcely any accent, though his tone of voice did betray his astonishment.

'You want to remain among us?'

'If you would allow me.'

'But we're very poor. We've nothing but our huts and a few small sailing boats.'

'That would suit me perfectly.'

'We've had a few Europeans visit us, but none of them has ever wanted to stop at Mouli—You'll be the first.'

'I'll be proud of that—I want nothing better.'

'In that case, you're welcome.'

11 *Mouli: Island at the End of the World*

THE *Nautical Instructions* describe an atoll in these words:

An atoll is a coral formation emerging from the sea and most often assuming the shape of a wreath. Within the wreath is a lagoon. Islets covered with vegetation develop on the wreath, sometimes isolated and sometimes as a continuous chain, so that, in this case, the wreath may appear as a long wooded girdle. Islets of the same formation may be found inside the lagoon. If there are no such islets, or if they do not exist nearby, one must expect to find numerous coral bushes in the lagoon.

In many of the atolls the wreath remains fragmented, thus allowing the lagoon to communicate freely with the ocean. The channels or passages of communication are of the most varied depths. Sometimes they are accessible to the largest vessels, sometimes they are hardly navigable by the light native craft. One must, therefore, not venture into them without taking the most careful precautions.

Referring particularly to Ouvéa:

The atoll of Ouvéa (or Uvéa) is formed on the east by the island of Ouvéa; to the north and south by two chains of islets, masses of coral for the most part subjected to much pounding by the ocean, and covered with vegetation; there are the Uenéti islets—separated from the island of Ouvéa by a channel about a hundred yards wide; and then, to the south-east, Mouli.

About Mouli we learn:

This is the best and most sheltered anchorage in the lagoon, with depths of from about four and a half to six fathoms and a bed where the sand is thickest. One is nearer to the land than elsewhere and sheltered from south-east, southerly and south-west winds. The beach is of easy access for vessels. Water can be found in wells situated some thirty yards from the strand, but the water is always brackish. Anchorage is less than half a mile from land (for large vessels or those of medium tonnage). Bearings may be taken on the church situated to the south. The axis of the avenue of coco-palms leading to it gives the alignment.

Nowhere else, as far as I know, has a line been written about Mouli. A pamphlet published by the government of New Caledonia and Dependencies does not describe Mouli, but says the following about Ouvéa:

Situated about eighty miles from the eastern coast of New Caledonia, the atoll of Ouvéa (not to be confused with the island of Ouvéa in the Wallis group) is of coral formation and consists of a main island, Fayawe (formerly called Ouvéa)—where lives a gendarme who acts as Resident— together with some secondary islands (Uenéti, Mouli) and some uninhabited islets disposed in an irregular circle round the lagoon. The climate is particularly healthy, the coconut plantations are flourishing and the population, of Polynesian origin, is very friendly.

Imagine an immense jade-coloured lagoon under a sun high in the heavens. The isles and islets which girdle the lagoon are not visible from each other across the expanse of water. Toward the south-east a thick plantation of coco-palms lines a crescent of dazzling sand, then the beach gives way to a charming landscape of wooded rock overlooking the passage that communicates with the open sea. Set back a little from the passage, a few small gaily painted cutters are quietly anchored.

On the beach a fishing-net is spread out across a few stakes. In the sparse shade of a solitary coco-palm a horse, attached by a rusty chain, turns to avoid the sun. The blows of a carpenter's axe ring out, and you can hear the squawkings of chickens as the dogs run after them. Women in ample, multi-coloured robes come to draw water from the well among the sands. Then they go off again, chattering, toward the village. Smoke rises above the green foliage of the tall coco-palms that mask everything but the tip of the church's white spire.

Once you are through the edge of this pretty plantation, you find a collection of about fifty huts on the sandy soil. They are surrounded by out-buildings and the largest is the chief's dwelling. Rectangular, square or round (in the latter case having a very pointed, conical roof), other huts are of various dimensions according to the size of the family they shelter. All are made exclusively of natural, vegetable materials. Between the huts wind small paths entirely covered with dried palm-leaves which make a rustling carpet under the lightest step. This covering is renewed when needful by a few strokes with a matchet on the leaves of the neighbouring trees. Other trees give shade and coolness: flame-trees, filaos, bread-trees, papaws and bananas. The gigantic taro leaves spread out wide at the foot of clumps of hibiscus and bougainvillea. Delicate sand-lilies lead towards the beach. That is Mouli: two hundred and fifty inhabitants at the end of the world. Mouli, Pierre Dumai translated for me from the dialect, 'the last island before the great passage'.

12 Origins

'OUR ancestors were Wallisians,' declared Pierre Dumai emphatically. 'That's not a legend, that's a fact.'

Round about him, in the half-light of his hut, heads nodded in agreement.

One of the women listening silently on the threshold got up, walked round the circle of men squatting on pandanus-leaf mats, and went to turn up the smoky wick of the paraffin lamp that was our assembly's only light. Outside, the still coco-palms stood out against the moonlit night.

The tragedy that led to the Polynesian, or rather, Wallisian peopling of Mouli was recounted to me that evening:

More than twenty generations ago, on the island of Ouvéa (Wallis), a prince went with his young son to pay a visit to the king in his palace at Natautou. The prince was hoping to settle a legal dispute so serious that it threatened to lead to fighting. The king had a son of the same age as the prince's, and, during the audience, the two children were left together outside the palace. When the interview was over, the prince came out and looked for his son. He found him standing petrified with horror before the bloody body—unconscious, perhaps even dead—of the king's son. The two children had been fighting: they had taken up their fathers' quarrel.

No one had yet noticed the tragedy. The prince knew all too well that he and his son would die if the king thought they were guilty. How could they clear themselves? The prince urged his son back to their village, and the notables were called together. They all agreed the king's wrath would spare no one, and that he would not listen to the story that his own son had first insulted and then struck the other boy, who had only defended himself.

Death hovered over the village. They must all flee. A soothsayer stood up in the assembly and predicted that canoes would carry the men in the direction of the setting sun and that their salvation would be at hand as soon as they caught sight of clouds of white birds. Canoes were hastily launched, and for most of their crews the prophecy was fulfilled. Some of the boats were lost and in others men died when their supplies of dried bananas and fresh water had been exhausted, but the survivors one morning saw white birds, and then soon the land where they put ashore.

They were so weak that the inhabitants of the island could have massacred them without resistance, and this was perhaps one of the reasons why they were well received and looked after. Quickly enough the Wallisians got back their strength and fraternized with their saviours. They baptized the atoll 'Ouvéa', and increased and multiplied with wives from among the black-skinned natives. Soon the Wallisian strain predominated and the children were born with the light skins of their ancestors from over the sea.

'One of the companions of the prince who fled from Wallis was called Dumai,' concluded the Great Chief, 'and that is why, since his conquest of Mouli, we have been chiefs from father to son.'

This Polynesian ancestry explained the remarkable hospitality shown me, and the mildness and intelligence displayed by the guests at this first meal. About ten notables, making up the Council of Elders, had taken part in a dinner of coco-palm kernels, fish and boiled yams. They varied in age from thirty-five to seventy, as far as I could judge, though they all seemed to possess an astonishing youthfulness of body—even those whose hair was snow-white. With the exception of one, the youngest, they seemed kindly, peaceable people and showed astonishment at my slightest remarks—as I did, in fact, at theirs. As to the man whose attitude was in such marked contrast to that of all the others, I was to learn later that his behaviour was just what was expected of him. Génio (for that was his name) had a peculiar job—that of constant criticism and contradiction of the Great Chief. This explained his cutting tone and what had seemed to me his arrogance: it was apparently an official attitude incumbent on his position.

Pierre Dumai informed me that the next day 'the word' would be pronounced regarding me and he asked me, in the tribe's name, to be good enough to be present at the ceremony. Then we took leave of one another. So brilliant was the night that I had no need of my electric torch to find the hut they had put at my disposal.

'a procession of men and women carrying the other half of the devil'
' "Chopé. Chopé" '
'the shoreward ends of the devil being pulled in'

13 The Word

There is no doubt that Hitler had a power of fascinating men.
                                                Winston Churchill.

EVERY writer knows how greatly the transcribing of thoughts forces him to adopt a precision the spoken word does not possess. Before the missionaries introduced into Mouli the writing of French, all knowledge, all law, all the restraints imposed by convention, were communicated by the human voice alone: oral tradition. We cannot imagine how our ancestors in preliterate ages managed to avoid the errors of communication by word of mouth alone. However, the fore-fathers of the present-day Mouli tribe discovered the ideal method.

Not far from the church square and right at the end of a flower-decked lane leading steeply up from the beach, there is a little whitewashed house—rather pathetic in its decay—which serves as the school. Here a native of the island, educated at Nouméa, teaches the French language. It is astonishingly well learnt and written with remarkable perfection by the children.

The Word is celebrated on a clearing of hard irregular ground in front of the church. It is arranged in an extra-ordinarily wise fashion. The speaker—who is either the chief or one of the notables—informs the members of the tribe of matters of general interest, and the audience *turns its back upon the orator*. Thus, since they do not see the man who is addressing them, no one is influenced by his magnetism, no one fears his flashing eyes, or is impressed by his mimicry, his gestures, his impetuousness, or the grandiloquence of his invective.

'the fish laid out on the sand were still showing some signs of life'
'red or silver snappers with spatulate mouths'
'Chop-Chop, the old mongrel, seized an enormous file-fish by the head'

Nothing can be conveyed by attitudenizing. Nothing counts but the word, its truth, its accuracy, its correctness. And those who *really* listen, with every sense except hearing in repose, are much more able to pay attention, to concentrate, to discern. The facts are stripped of all that masks their nakedness. Error is quickly detected, exaggeration is useless, lying impossible. The orator can convince no one except by the strict intrinsic worth of what is *solely heard*.

More than that, the man who submits to such a custom, by renouncing all the tinsel and finery of eloquence restores to the art of speaking something of its significance and grandeur. If this custom had been spread to the rest of the world, the course of history might have been changed.

'What's Pierre saying,' I asked in a low voice of one of the Elders sitting near me, with his right hand cupped around his ear.

'He says it's the first time a European has come to stay among us at Mouli.'

Like every able-bodied member of the tribe, gathered on the wide, sandy slope with their backs to Pierre Dumai, I listened to his thrilling voice, with its imperious undertones. He was speaking in the Mouli language. Most of the women shaded themselves from the sun by holding taro leaves above their wavy heads of hair. Even the youngest children were silent, respectful, attentive.

'We must welcome him like a brother,' went on translating the Elder to me. 'We must build him a hut and celebrate a great *bugna* in his honour.'

As the Great Chief's speech went on, although I could not understand one word of it, it seemed to me that I was only then making acquaintance with Dumai, discovering his personality. The voice that I heard, without seeing the man who emitted it, revealed to me his most secret self. The tones, the inflexions expressed not only the thought but the deep nature of the man's character.

'Pierre says he's proud you've chosen Mouli, after seeing so many other islands, to stay with us,' whispered the Elder. 'He's saying what you said last night at the big house: "There is no other place like Mouli in all the South Pacific." He says these are the same words the Dumai ancestors used when they fought to conquer our island.'

So the Great Chief saw his ancestors' choice confirmed by me. If Mouli had been selected as the site of Austral Paradise by a foreigner who had travelled widely, well, that was a proof the island really was just that. Had I not been all around the world? Was I not well qualified to make comparisons? There could not be the slightest doubt about Pierre Dumai's sincerity or about the real warmth of his welcome—and he had communicated his own sentiments to the whole tribe. We could not foresee what would be the result of all this, but that mattered little. They had adopted me and I had adopted them.

During the night, as I lay on the pallet in my hut, I felt deeply happy and proud, at peace with the whole world. But then came memories and with them some slight sadness. I thought of the inhibitions which in the past had checked that sort of spontaneous outburst to which I owed my present happiness—most probably from fear of being snubbed by strangers. But, then, I had been living in a conditioned society, conditioned by restraints; maybe that was the real reason for my inhibitions.

I was soon to find out that the new society in which I was beginning to feel myself at home was ruled by very precise social laws. It was not a harsh revelation of something which I had always thought of as the inhuman attitude of the West. 'Ignorance of the Law is no excuse.' Everyone knew these rules. What I was to discover was a real religion of human relations.

14 Opposition : Constitution

NOTHING would have made me suggest it myself, but I was relieved by Génio's suggestion that we stay where we were for a little while before going back to the village. A walk of several miles under the burning sun had dried me out and I was dying of thirst. The horse began to nibble at the short grass that grew in scanty clumps, and the sack of yams and the load of sugar-cane slipped about on his spine and his sweat-soaked flanks. Génio came down from the palm where he had gathered a few nuts. At one gulp I swallowed the juice of one he held out to me. Then he drank and came and sat down in the shade of the filaos. We were near the edge of the cliff and could gaze over the immense expanse of the sea. Far off, women loaded with faggots were making their way where the wet sand offered the best hold for their broad, naked feet. The sky was intensely blue, more luminous still than the lagoon's dull green, absolutely motionless surface.

I hesitated a long while before asking, 'You're Pierre's enemy?'

He looked at me with astonishment and then burst out laughing.

'Not on your life!'

'That first evening at the chief's house, I was surprised to hear you oppose him.'

'That's true, I did oppose him, but that doesn't mean I'm his enemy.'

Was there not something contradictory about that? He noticed the look of puzzlement on my face.

'Well, look. In all things we follow Custom. Custom dictates that if one man alone commands the tribe, he soon becomes inflated with pride, and that is bad for everyone. The important thing is not the will of one man but the interests of all the people. The ancients used to say, "It's better to have a great cyclone than an arrogant Big Chief: no one can prevent a cyclone from destroying things, but one can prevent a chief from becoming bad".'

'How?'

'He must be made to obey Custom.'

'And who's going to make him?'

'The Council of Elders—you've seen all the old men, Alphonse, Néophyte, Ignace, Mathias and the others? They are the Keepers of Custom.'

'And you?'

'Me? Well, it's like this. A thing looks like day to one man and like night to another; but maybe the thing is really like twilight: so Custom decrees that there should be always a man opposed to the Big Chief, who argues about his wishes. And that's me. For instance, suppose Pierre is speaking before the Elders and he is saying something of importance for the tribe. I put in my word and say what I'd do if I was in Pierre's place—always the opposite, or in a different way. Then, well, the rest of the Elders see clearly if Pierre's right.'

'In fact you're the leader of the Opposition.'

'That's it, if you like, the leader of the Opposition. But remember, Bernard, I was chosen also because everyone thinks that I could become the Big Chief if unfortunately Pierre was no longer worthy. So Pierre knows well enough that I'm not his enemy, that all I'm doing is to obey Custom; and also that he's not the only man who could lead the tribe.'

'Pierre is the hereditary chief? He is descended from the Dumais, chiefs from father to son, and Iviki will be chief in his turn?'

'Yes, but note this very carefully, very carefully indeed: it is always the Council of Elders which decides—that's to say, we respect the family whose ancestors were leaders

85

because they were the most worthy of leading, it wouldn't be right to deprive the descendant of his position as Big Chief, but he's got to prove that he himself respects his ancestors and that he is both energetic and wise; in other words, that he acts always in accordance with Custom.'

'All right, but suppose that the Big Chief disobeys Custom?'

'The Council of Elders may decide he should not any longer be our chief. But that would be only if he committed very grave mistakes, and committed them repeatedly.'

'So he might make one serious error without risking anything?'

Génio raised his forefinger and wagged his hand rapidly.

'Not on your life! Every fault must be expiated. He's punished.'

'How? By whom? By a court of law?'

'The Council of Elders decides. If Pierre's behaved badly, Benoît thrashes him. He must beat him severely if he deserves it, not so hard if the sin is not so serious.'

'Would Pierre allow himself to be beaten?'

'He must submit, otherwise he would only make his fault worse. Custom says that he's not a god, but a man like all the others, and that he may well make mistakes, but—note this—like everyone else he must pay for his mistakes and accept punishment.'

I could imagine the lusty Benoît punishing Pierre and then going back to his carpentering.

'And wouldn't Pierre be ashamed of this? It must be difficult to be beaten, and everyone to know it, and then to go on being chief.'

'Maybe in his inmost being he would feel ashamed, but a real Big Chief takes up command again at once and shows no signs of shame—not just from pride, but to prove that he's paid for his fault and that it exists no more. He's rid of it, it's finished, everyone forgets it. The rest of the tribe will then see he's not arrogant, but strong, here and here'—Génio

pointed to his heart and his forehead—'and they'll respect him
as though nothing had happened.'

'And wouldn't Pierre bear a grudge against Benoît?'

'Never on your life! Benoît would never strike Pierre for
any personal reason, but only in obedience to Custom, and
Pierre knows this quite well. A little later Benoît would call
on Pierre. They would drink together and Benoît would make
friendly and respectful remarks. The devil is cast out, finished
off! If the weather is right for fishing, he will go out and catch
a turtle, or a napoleon, or even a carangue—they are called
"chief's fish". And even if Benoît only managed to catch
other fish, Pierre would know that Benoît had wanted to
catch the others and offer them as a present. That's our Custom,
Bernard. No, not on your life, I'm not Pierre's enemy, and
you'll see that if you attend some of our meetings. I'll oppose
Pierre, but not as an enemy.'

We got up. With a slash of his matchet Génio sliced off the
end of a sugar-cane that was sticking out of the load. He
offered it to me and I chewed on the fibrous stalk as we took
the pathway, overgrown with lily-stems, that runs along beside
the graveyard to the village.

Travel Notes An hereditary power subject to the control
of an assembly of Wise Men. A Senate with executive
functions [Benoît]. The President's opinion always ques-
tioned by the Opposition, which Opposition is recognized
as an institution and has a sort of mouthpiece. This arrange-
ment automatically induces discussion and just as automatically confers on the Elders alone the status of judges.
In other places the Constitution only is all-powerful: here
Custom. It is a combination of constitutional monarchy,
legislature and executive, a democracy with apparently no
suffrage. There must be something else of the same sort—I
must find out.

Pierre Dumai told me tonight that they will build my hut
tomorrow.

15 *A Palace of Palms*

PIERRE DUMAI had served morning tea in the courtyard of his dwelling and then, under his orders, the team got ready to build my hut. There were twelve men and as many women. While the women cut fresh palm-leaves, the men went off among the trees, which had already been marked, and lopped off stakes, cross-bars, beams and slats. These they laid down systematically on the building-site. Later the men could pick up these components, all of regular, traditional size, and fix them into their right places.

Other men were tearing down and softening up lianas of various thicknesses and these also were laid down so that they were exactly at hand to strengthen or fit together the joints of the building. Other men still were piling the rustling, dry palm leaves that are always kept ready for making roofs. During these preparations the women were plaiting the green palm-leaves into the solid and tough rectangular panels which would form the walls.

From ancient times a complete building plan had been handed down, perfected in every detail so that from start to finish the most officious foreman would have been unable to note a minute wasted. I watched with astonishment. A hut is built by community spirit: the co-ordinated movements were so efficient as to seem almost miraculous. Tropical stakhanovists they were, but their aim was not to produce more and more, but to turn out the best possible product at the price of the least effort. Never any hurry, an appearance almost of indolence, an ease of movement of perfect precision—the result of a very long training.

Soon, everything was ready for the second phase of the

88

'there were more than thirty of us in Benoît's little boat'
overleaf: 'a gigantic, armour-plated spider'

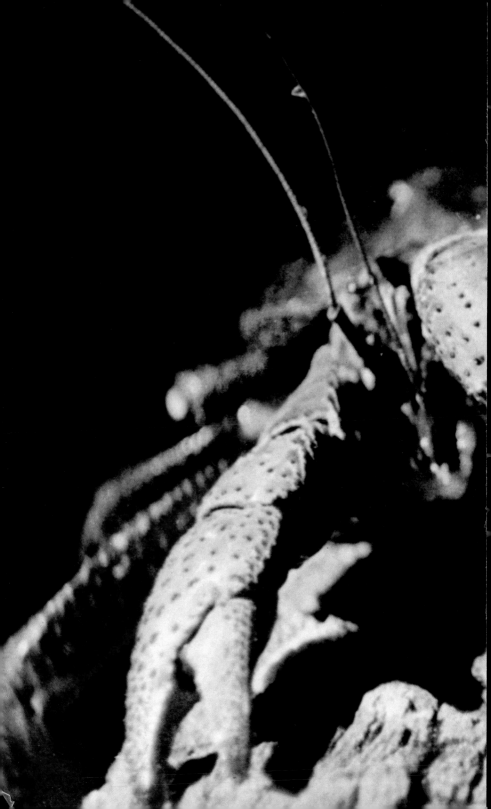

operations. The tools consisted of matchets, a sort of huge, polished wooden needle some three feet long, and very unripe (and so heavy) coconuts. A length was stripped off their fibrous covering so that it could be wound round the first and middle fingers, thus affording a secure hold. Everyone was at his appointed post. On an order from Pierre the hut arose from the ground as though by magic. Some of the quaint music that accompanies cartoon films would have gone marvellously well with this fairy-tale of a man watching his vegetal house literally rising before his eyes. Hardly was the rectangular skeleton in place before the roof took shape over the cross-slats. Three thicknesses of dry palm-leaves were sewn together in a sloping cover. The needle's eye was threaded with a liana half as thick as a man's finger and every eight inches the needle pierced a perfectly regular, clean hole. The supervisor of this roofing flattened the seam with heavy blows from a coconut and the edges were trimmed with matchets. The thick thatch would never allow through any rain and would keep the inside of the hut as cool as possible. While all this was going on the panels of green palm leaves for the walls were fixed in place and lashed together. All were of exactly the same size and their surfaces as smooth as if they had been cut by machine. A door, for which no lock was necessary, completed this apparently effortless masterpiece—my palace of palms.

I did not know where to look. I was delighted even more than I was astonished.

'mats of banana leaves were decorated with vegetables and on this bed other food was placed'
'they held their cards as though they were weapons'

16 The Coco-palm Crabs

'TEN slabs of chewing-gum for a coconut crab.'

I had certainly pronounced these words to Iviki after my siesta when he had come to give me some sea-shells. I then discovered, at my expense maybe, that Radio Coco Junior functioned with formidable efficiency. The great news seemed to have run round the whole tribe in a matter of minutes. There, in front of my hut, was assembled a wild gang of more than twenty children, daubed with vegetable dyes, grimy with wet sand, wearing garlands of little red and yellow flowers or even of turtle eggs. They were all eager to start hunting as soon as night fell.

Now I recklessly had not checked the contents of the few boxes of provisions I had taken off the boat (and before I had got those which I had asked Colliard to send me by the next copra schooner, which might touch at Ouvéa no one knew when). So had I not given a promise I could not keep? Would I have enough chewing-gum for everyone? It was nearly the end of a balmy day. Well, it could not be helped, we should see what we should see. I stuffed my shorts' pockets with all the precious slabs I could find and we set off to a place a good way away from the village, where the older among the children hoped to find plenty of the crabs, although they are very wary and comparatively rare.

Much has been talked about the subterranean coconut crabs of the Pacific, but you never see one except in curio shops, where there may be a prehistoric crab full of formol, varnished and covered with dust, in the window next to bolts of *parāu* cloth, carved mother-of-pearl and stuffed globe-fish mounted as bedside lamps. What I was hoping was that our hunting

would be good without being too good. I had got enough to
pay for fourteen of these strange creatures that emerge at night
from their lairs deep down in the earth to crack open windfall
coconuts or those still on the trees—their only food.

We passed the cemetery and advanced in Indian file on a
little sandy path running along the top of the cliffs.

Everyone gathered the dry palm-leaves scattered on the
ground, twisting them into torches and lighting them at a fire
of twigs. Then, accompanied by the crackling of sparks and
the chirring of insects, we plunged into the weird shadows of
the palm-grove—a procession of lunar beings on alien soil,
silently searching . . . the rustle of palm-leaves underfoot . . .
other leaves, armfuls of them, were lighted at torches
three-quarters burnt . . . whispers . . . the scuttling of a
rodent.

Then suddenly one of the children cried out and rushed
forward with outstretched hands. The creature he had just
sighted outside its lair would have alarmed many adults, but
the children seized the crab and put a stop to its nightmarish
movements. Imagine a gigantic spider, sprouting two long,
flexible antennae and armed with enormous claws, enclosed in
a bristling, knobby shell.

Another child, not ten years old, and then a third, rushed
after other monsters. Tender hands grasped the plated cuirasses
of the dazzled creatures. Slender, agile fingers wormed their
way into the sockets between the hairy, clawed legs clinging to
palm-roots or scurrying on the ground, while monstrous,
wavy pincers tried to crush the empty air. The children picked
spider-crabs from the ground and used them to threaten one
another as a game. They would push a bit of wood between
the claws and slowly the crab would cut it through. Then
these hunter children would amuse themselves by teasing the
crabs with their fingers but well out of reach. They bound the
horrid creatures with lianas and baptized them most ir-
reverently with the names of Elders or old women of the

tribe. If they attempted to get back into their holes a slight tap would soon discourage them.

The children also chose slanting palm-trees, took the coconut-crabs to the roots and then urged them to climb up. They were highly amused to watch the crabs' slow and laborious upward progress—sometimes helped by a push on their heavy, spider-like bellies that protruded behind them like purple water-skins. Then the boys would hold one end of the liana-leash between their teeth and also work up the tree, soon outdistancing the heavy, clumsy crabs. Once at the top the children would call out to the crabs and throw them bits of bark. When the creatures caught up, their captors picked their claws one at a time from the trunk and dropped them so that they hung like armed pendulums, wriggling hideously.

'Eight, nine, ten, that's all.'

The last of the crabs, skilfully trussed, was pushed down to join the others in a jute sack. I was solvent. A circle of spluttering, newly-lighted torches lit up the scene of the pay-out. Then the biggest boy—who had carefully counted the bits of chewing-gum—divided them equally among everyone present. Another boy hoisted the sack on his shoulder and we set off home.

17 Sharing

Men who had made five thousand, the year before last, and ten thousand last year were urging on nerve-yelping bodies and parched brains so that they might make twenty thousand this year; and the men who had broken down immediately after making their twenty thousand dollars were hustling to catch trains, to hustle through the vacations which the hustling doctors had ordered.

Sinclair Lewis: *Babbitt*

THERE is a terrible saying: *Man is born, lives and dies alone.* A saying matched by Sartre's bitter remark, *Hell is other people.* The idea of society, of community, splits the world with ideological struggles. Somewhere in the realm of divine mathematics maybe there is a mistake in a decimal point. Or, perhaps, since the purposes of God are inscrutable, the miserable imperfection of our dislocated world is caused by the birth-pangs of a splendid society to be?

But such speculations is idle. For the present we are at the other end of the world, at the Antipodes, in the company of men who have met together at night for the give and take of conversation. Sitting on the plaited pandanus mats that cover the floor of the Mouli Big House, gathered around the great, soot-encrusted kettle on its bed of embers, there are, in addition to the Big Chief Pierre Dumai and his usual opponent Génio, a number of the Elders—the sturdy, easy-going Alphonse, with his shrewd eyes and contagious smile; the taciturn Mathias, with his short beard and snow-white hair—yet his body is absolutely that of a young man, reminiscent, despite his sixty-three, sixty-four or sixty-five years, of some contemplative Arcadian shepherd; there is the imperturbable Benoît, wearing his usual, old battered Anzac felt hat; then there is Néophyte, a humble man, despite his huge, rough-hewn frame and great bulging muscles. Old Ignace looks as though he could not sit still more than a minute, he is so full of nervous energy, and his spare, Asiatic face reveals his love of discussion. Julien, reserved as always, has on his long, deeply lined features an expression of close and solemn attention. Then there is Victor, the baker, expansive and cheerful, who stammers a little. A few very old men complete the company, one of them blind: they had to lead him and help him sit down, but his sightless eyes do not detract from the smiling serenity of his wrinkled face.

'Maybe we are kindly, as you say, Bernard,' Pierre remarked in reply to my speech of thanks and gratitude for the hut. 'But if this is so, it's the Custom that has made us a good people. We must always obey Custom and it is good, very good, for all of us.' There was a general murmur of approval.

'You came here as a stranger and we admitted you among us. Now we act towards you according to Custom. We will give you nothing extra, we will simply share with you what we have. What is mine is yours, and I'll give it to you if you need it. That's Custom.'

'For instance,' broke in Benoît, 'you may want to explore our lagoon and you've not got a boat. Benoît or Néophyte will lend you their boat—there's your boat.'

(Néophyte looked at me and made motions of hoisting a sail. Benoît bowed his head in approval.)

'If they need their boats to go fishing, well, then they'll ask you for them back, but you can go fishing with them if you like and they'll share the catch with you. Everyone will do the same, with yams or taros or anything else you've need of and you haven't got. And you must do the same.'

Pierre held out his arm and made a sweeping gesture.

'Our island belongs to us, and it belongs to everyone. Each family needs a place for its hut and some land for a garden.

There are some families that have more than others, but that's only because they have more children and old people to feed. If the head of a family is ill, or if he has to do work that prevents him from looking after his patch properly, then someone else will go and till his land so that his family will have enough to eat. For instance, there's Alphonse, who is a very good mason and he had to spend many days building the well: well, a young man from another family went and harvested Alphonse's yams for him.'

Alphonse pulled a funny face and nodded.

'I had my yams harvested, but everyone can go and take water from the well.'

'Supposing there's an old woman left all alone,' said Néophyte. 'Her old man's dead, and her son, well, everyone will bring her something to eat, all she needs in fact. If she gets sick she will be nursed.'

'For instance,' put in Ignace, before Néophyte could go on, 'when there was the big cyclone—and remember, more than half the huts were blown away—well, those who had no home went and stayed with those who had, and then all of us set to work to put up new huts. No one among us need worry about being without a roof or without food, never in your life. Everyone's got what he needs—or no one has.'

'Like brothers,' I said.

'It's Custom that makes us brothers,' said Ignace.

Victor was obviously burning to speak:

'It's good to ggggo to Nouméaaa sometimes to travel but aaafterwards it's ggggood to get back to Moumoumouli.'

The Elders nodded their assent.

'With us, no rich, no poor, that's Custom,' declared Pierre.

'All right, that goes for lodging, for food, but you've got to have things which you can only get with money—lamp-oil, clothes, tools, tobacco, rope. . . . How do you manage?'

'We've got copra. Everyone must work on the copra crop.

When we've sold it, we share out the money or barter perhaps with firms at Nouméa, and we share the proceeds.'

'Copra's enough to cover all your needs?'

'No, not always, it depends on the crop, and also on the price. When that's low we can't pay for everything.'

'So what?'

'Well, some of the tribe go off and work at Nouméa.'

'The fathers and mothers of families,' Génio added.

'Why those especially?'

'Fathers and mothers of families working at Nouméa get family allowances, and that makes more money.'

'You share out the money too?'

'We share everything. The fathers and mothers of families spend as little as possible and send the rest to the tribe. That's Custom.'

'And if someone wants to have more than the others and not share and share alike?'

I could realize by the dead silence how improper my question was. Such an eventuality was inconceivable. Could any member of the tribe be capable of such a heinous crime?

'Impossible,' said Benoît at last. 'Every man's hand would be against him. No one would help him in his work, he would be all alone. He'd be done for.'

'We would cast him out, it would be worse than death!'

There was silence again.

You share. You share everything. Custom is proof against misery and solitude. The islanders wanted nothing else, except *in common*.

'they wriggled beside the red flames and the dresses clinging to their bodies soon dried out'

18 Fishing with the Devil

Ancestral fears arise anew in the hearts of men as they walk in the coco-groves during moonless nights. It is the devil that spies on them and makes the palm-leaves rustle. Maybe men, before they became men, were fish, since these have fear of the slightest sound. And that is why the Ancients called a 'devil' the great net of lianas and palm-leaves which, when it is shaken in the waters, frightens fish so much.

Translated from a Melanesian Legend.

IVIKI ran through the darkness and the torrential rain and came into the Big House.

'Rain-water's not good for a little mackerel like you,' Benoît shouted at him.

The men on the mats smiled at the sight of the shivering Iviki. He wiped his naked body and his dripping hair with the bit of *paräu* he had untied from round his middle, squeezing out the cloth several times. He stood looking at his father in an attitude of mute supplication. The child's beautiful, intelligent face, its marvellously delicate features and the great, dark eyes expressed respect, even fear—but also an ardent desire he should be allowed to remain. With a short nod Pierre Dumai gave permission and Iviki, silently, though beaming with joy, went and crouched by his father. Old Mathias was near the square hearth and he raised the kettle from its bed and poured out the boiling, very sweet tea into an enamel bowl, which Néophyte held out to the child.

'It's better at Fayawa,' old Ignace declared sententiously, as he sliced a bit off his plug of tobacco.

'Beware the current,' said Benoît. 'You remember the last time, the devil broke at Fayawa.'

'the giant clam's flesh is a delicacy the men of Mouli procure in a very ingenious fashion'

'It was the moon for a strong tide,' replied Benoît with feeling, 'and the devil broke because there were not enough of us.'

'This time everyone will be there,' declared Pierre Dumai. 'Everyone—old women and children as well.'

'You've got to be very careful at the Great Reef. It's always the same story'—Ignace imitated an animal taking cover—'lots of fish will hide in the holes and the women will get tired walking on the coral.'

Provided that the weather allowed them to take advantage of this favourable moon, what was the most suitable place for the great fishing planned for the next day? The discussion was one that had recurred throughout the centuries.

On the south-west, with green lianas at the foot of low cliffs, the Fayawa passage is a long vein of blue water, shallow, with a bed of coral sand. To the south the passage leads into the ocean, and to the north runs into the vast lagoon. At low tide a man can walk across the passage and only be out of his depth in the middle. But at high tide, when the current is running strong, no one could walk or even swim across. He would be swept along like a straw.

To the north-east, the Great Reef is a vast curved plateau exposed at low tide and swarming with fish, but its jagged surface makes it very difficult to perform a complicated manoeuvre with more than two hundred people. Despite the strong current such a manoeuvre was much easier at the Fayawa passage. Moreover, no one could deny that over three tons of fish had been taken there about twenty years before.

Ignace placed a little square of dry banana leaf on his knobbly knees, crumbled his black tobacco between the palms of his hands, arranged the morsels very carefully on the leaf, which he wetted along the edge with his saliva and then lighted with an ember. When he had finished this ceremony he resumed his detailed argument in favour of Fayawa.

'And be very careful at the Big Reef. If there are sharks there, they'll be large ones.'

'Ignace, you damned old rogue,' teased Néophyte. 'You're frightened your old woman will give you hell if you make her walk on the coral where there's big sharks. You fool, if a shark makes a meal of her, all to the good. Then you'll be a young man again and ready to take on a new wife.'

Everyone laughed. Ignace's wife was an upstanding old girl well known for her gift of the gab and her physical strength. Ignace pulled down his mouth contemptuously and then lowered his head and gave it knowing little shakes. Everyone knew well enough that Néophyte was not always master in his own house.

The huge thatch rocked under a blast of wind and the rain pattered heavily on the roof. Coconuts were blown from the trees and thudded on to the soaked soil.

'We'll decide tomorrow, depending on the weather,' said Pierre Dumai.

Mathias bowed his head in agreement. Pierre turned and looked at me.

'The weather is master.'

'The weather's master. That's the truth,' Génio echoed. Up to now he had said nothing, but he had followed the discussion with close attention. As nothing Pierre had said aroused the slightest controversy, he had kept quiet.

Time had come for the meeting to break up. I pushed out into the rain and ran on the slippery palm-leaves into the warm dampness of my hut.

I opened one eye. Iviki was silhouetted in my doorway. My feet were sticking out from under the *paräu* and he threw a little pebble at them and burst out laughing. Suddenly I remembered the disagreeable whirring of an alarm-clock that I had meant for months to replace—no doubt in a former existence. Hell! I woke up completely, jumped from my bed, pulled on a pair of shorts and hurried out of the hut, still half-dazed. I followed Iviki to the edge of the coconut grove.

We were lucky. A diamond clarity spread across a perfectly clear sky. On the beach the Elders were chatting and groups of women and children stood near them. Young lads swam to the shore, pulling the boats so that everyone could easily get aboard.

Pierre Dumai waved to me as I ran up to him.

'It's Fayawa,' he shouted.

Men, women and children all crowded in together. There were more than thirty of us in Benoît's little boat, which led the merry race from Mouli. Guy, a tall young man of about twenty, sang all the time, accompanying himself on a guitar. He waved the guitar about at the people standing in the boats a few cables' length off. They were even more crowded than ours.

Eventually Benoît lowered his coarse, patched sail and it fell on a group of women. The keel bumped softly. Guy put down his guitar, went forward and prepared to cast anchor. His dog ran up and barked round his legs.

'Chop-Chop, go on, jump, jump.'

Iviki, standing beside me, burst out laughing at the sight of Guy pushing his old mongrel in the water. The poor dog was not at all keen to jump, though whimpering with impatience to reach the shore. But in he fell, splashing us, and then swam strongly with his bandy legs until he scrambled up on to the sand. He worried one of the many hermit-crabs with his bulbous, scarred snout, and then dashed off toward a bank of washed-up shells. A crab had the temerity to threaten him with its upraised claws and he tossed it several yards. Then leaving the crab, he rushed off to bark at some horses galloping along the cliff-path. The riders shouted shrilly and brandished their matchets. Half-way across the immense stretch of the beach, little groups of people, like dark dots, were hurrying to join us. Not an able-bodied adult had remained in the village and no child had been naughty enough to be punished by being left at home on this great occasion. (Though I am not sure that the children, the real lords of creation on Mouli, ever were punished.)

A very old man, standing upright and paddling his little dinghy, came through the passage towards our group—Pierre Dumai, Génio, Alphonse and Benoît, the leaders of the Fishing, and me. The west bank of the Fayawa passage belongs to the Mouli tribe, but the east bank is controlled by this Elder of the neighbouring Leikigné tribe, and they had seen our signals. Fishing is free in the passage, for sea fish belong to those who take the trouble to catch them, but on no account would this 'devil fishing' have been decided on without the old borderer having been asked for his permission.

The chiefs of the Fishing, with Génio and Pierre Dumai at their head, went to meet this very old Elder and hauled up his boat on the bank. Each gave him the customary present of a packet or a plug of tobacco, and shook hands with all the marks of friendship and deepest respect. Pierre presented me to this robust old man of seventy-five. His eyes, under very prominent eyebrows, were lively and piercing. He spoke no French. Without taking his eyes from me, with his large, bony hands he clasped mine—and my present. Under this friendly pressure I hardly noticed how deformed and hard his hands were. It was only a formality no doubt, many times repeated; but accomplished as though something quite new and spontaneous.

The venerable Elder listened with attention to the leaders of the Fishing explain why they had chosen this time and place. Then Pierre asked him for permission to hold the great Fishing in the waters which separated two friendly tribes. Would the Elder also do the men of Mouli the honour of presiding over the Fishing? Although his bearing remained grave the old man could ill conceal his lively satisfaction at this observance of Customary Law. He accepted Pierre's offer and then, with a sweeping movement of his outstretched arms toward the passage, he indicated that it was free. Pierre then turned round and, facing those who were waiting in the shade of the wild coco-palms, he made the same gesture as the Elder.

The making of the devil could begin.

The women sang as they set to work to cut leaves from the palms and pile them up in heaps. The men, with strange, guttural cries, slashed their matchets in the undergrowth near the cliff. They tore at lianas and others hauled them out. The lianas they gathered were about as thick as a man's thumb and some of them were more than fifty feet long. Green coconuts were used as hammers and anvils. They were peeled quite smooth and employed to crush the ends of the lianas very carefully, so that they could be securely attached to one another. The fibrous substance of the ends had to be made very supple so that it could be firmly knotted, but not to be so weakened that the points of junction give way under the strain they were soon to bear. The success of the whole operation might be jeopardized by a single defective knot.

When it was joined up, the cordage was stretched out between two palm trunks in lengths of about one hundred yards. This was to be the cable, the support around which would be rolled palm-leaves split in two down the rib. This produced a kind of long, rustling curtain, about three feet high. To this other lengths would be added until they made up each of the devil's two parts, both about a thousand yards long. The final operation, the tying together of these two halves, would take place in the middle of the passage when the fish were surrounded—a hundred or a thousand of them, depending on the moon, and on the skill with which the manoeuvre was effected.

Both men and women worked deliberately, but with well co-ordinated movements and no trace of strain or of effort. Everything they did was marked by an ease and grace even the oldest still retained. These were skills handed down from ancestors, skills I had already seen when my hut was being built. It seemed, indeed, that the making of the great net of plants was the exercise of some natural power comparable with making trees grow, or leaves bud, or fruit ripen. In the shade of coco-palms, by the banks of the blue-water passage, there was being enacted a kind of medieval epic poem deriving straight from the source of life itself.

Benoît, who up to now had been fully occupied watching the tide, came over to see how things were progressing. He said they must all hurry, and then went back to his post. Less than half an hour later he walked over once more to tell the leaders of the Fishing that the time had come to lay the two parts of the devil on the bank.

'They'll be ready in a few minutes? Fine.' He had seen a school of *dawas*[1] and also a large ray followed by its young.

'That's it. Here they come,' yelled out one of the Elders to the young men about him. They emerged from the shade of palm and filao foliage to join the old men who had been attentively watching the final stages of the preparations from the beach. Far away, toward the reef in the open sea, a procession of men and women had just formed up carrying the other half of the devil.

Benoît threw a dry palm-leaf into the current and watched it float lazily along. Soon it would be slack water. The people of the upstream group were waiting for the signal. They were tiny, dark specks against the intense blue backcloth of the ocean that stretched far away beyond the barrier reef. Near us the downstream group waited on the wet sand quite near the lagoon. Alphonse had climbed on to a spur of rock and was surveying the scene. He was in an excellent position to direct operations. Génio was liaison officer: he had already taken

---

(1) *Unicornis*, a scale-less fish whose skin is like that of young sharks. The *dawa* has a horn above the eyes and sharp spurs on the tail.

up his post on the bank between the two groups with a red *paräu* in his hands.

A very few of the men had stripped off their usual singlets of blue or white cotton embroidered on the front in red. None of the women stripped, though the more daring wore only their underclothes: most of them would go into the water wearing their oldest dresses as well. There were Mathias's wife, the gentle and smiling Sophie, aged fifty-six; Anastasie, lively and robust despite her fifty-nine years; and among the oldest—those with white hair—was Léocadie, smoking a cigarette rolled in a banana-leaf to while away the last minutes of waiting. Her knotty, bony arms emerged from the sleeves of her faded Mission dress trimmed with torn and yellowed lace.

Benoît looked up at Alphonse. Alphonse crossed his arms several times above his head. The moment was at hand. Benoît undid the *paräu* from his waist and waved it in the slight breeze. Génio, a long way away, did the same for the benefit of the upstream group. The little brown figures carrying the devil began to move. Then when they had reached the middle of the passage, the downstream group got moving in turn and, as they went into the water, unwound the gigantic snail of leaves they had rolled together on the bank.

From two hundred throats came the echo of Alphonse's distant cry: '*Chopé. Chopé.* Pull. Pull.'

It was a hard task. They had to walk in water that got deeper and deeper, keep straight and maintain a regular distance from their neighbours, at the same time as dragging along each his bit of the devil. '*Chopé. Chopé.*' The leaders of each group were now swimming. The two parallel lines would soon reach the opposite bank and block the passage.

Then something held up the advance. From where I was it was impossible to make sure what it was. I saw only that one woman was out of line and that her nearest neighbours were moving toward her. Was she feeling faint? Had a big fish or a shark brushed against her? Had she hurt her foot on

'all beribboned and in their Sunday best, many of them with their faces painted in bright colours; each prepared his place at the table'
overleaf: 'children from the banquet, and they were going to walk on their hands!'
overleaf: 'I can remember white dresses, and faces daubed with sand and blue chalk'

an unexpected coral bush? A great roar of impatience swelled up and then died down when the woman resumed her place and the two lines had begun to move forward again. '*Chopé. Chopé.*'

At a signal from Alphonse, relayed by both Benoît and Génio, the two lines began a circular movement to join up. Now it was clear that the leading bearers were under a great strain. It was as though they had to bend a long bar of metal. '*Chopé. Chopé.*' Little by little the distance between the ends of the two arcs shortened—five hundred yards, four hundred, three hundred, two hundred . . . a hundred.

Now the state of the water changed. During the slack tide it had been quite smooth, but now the tide was turning: the face of the waters seemed to shudder. '*Chopé. Chopé. Chopé.*' There was still about fifty yards between the ends of the two halves. . . . Thirty, twenty, ten. . . . They stopped. It seemed hopeless, impossible to gain another yard. Swimming with all their strength they could just manage to hold the liana ends together with their outstretched arms, ready for them to be knotted together, but no headway. I could do nothing of any practical use, but I shouted encouragement. High above us, Alphonse's voice was now only a hoarse roar. '*Chopé. Chopé. Chopé.*'

From far off on the side wings, where they could only wait helplessly, men left their places and swam to help. It was several minutes before they could do anything and on either side of the gap the others were at the end of their tether; they could no longer hold their ground. Eventually the new arrivals relieved the distress somewhat. The men at the gap renewed their efforts and little by little the ends drew together. '*Chopé. Chopé. Chopé. Choooopé.*' Yes, they were going to meet. They met! Hands touched above the rushing water. Quickly they knotted the ends and made them fast. A great exultant shout arose. The devil was complete. With their heads bobbing around the half-circle they had just formed, two hundred human beings held fast the net of which they were a part.

inside: 'I was beginning to get adapted to the Mouli way of life'
'they took up their positions on the edge of the cliff'
'men went so far as to attack sharks, and that no bird can do'

High up above us, the sea-birds were already gathering. '*Chopé. Chopé. Chopé.*'

Now the shoreward ends of the devil were pulled in to drag the net towards land. Those near the bank took a sure foothold and hauled with all their might. I went and slipped in between Léocadie and a lad and pulled with them. She was mumbling something I did not understand and he went on chewing gum. '*Chopé. Chopé. Chopé.*' As they moved forward the swimmers shook the submerged palm-leaves. A momentary glitter on the blue water and a carangue leapt up. The current was running fast. We had to hurry. '*Chopé. Chopé. Chopé. Chooopé.*' Two, three more carangues leapt up.

Suddenly the devil broke. Two lengths of about two hundred yards each drifted away, sweeping along their astonished bearers. If it had been in the middle of the net and downstream, all would have been lost. But a knot at the end of the right wing had given way, upstream, in the direction of the current. It seemed that the swimmers were able to call on reserves of strength they had kept back for just such an emergency. Anyway, in a few minutes they repaired the damage. Once again the net was intact. '*Chopé. Chopé. Chopé.*'

The space between the carriers grew less as the devil's circumference shrank. As they felt it getting less and less heavy they shook more and more vigorously. The closer they moved to one another, and the nearer the shore, the more excited they became. A great arc of foam rose from the churning waters. An aiguillette shot up like a flying-fish within the devil. Another, upright on his tail, took off and then flopped down again on its enormous beak.

By the time the shoulders of the shouting men and women were almost touching, the splashing water rose well above their heads. '*Chopé. Chopé. Chopé.*' I kept on hauling and I stared and stared, but could as yet see nothing of the fish. But the children on shore with their sharp eyes had spotted them a long time before. They shouted and watched eagerly. At a peak-point of excitement there was Iviki clapping his hands and dancing for joy. '*Chopé. Chopé. Chopé.*' The din was infernal. Then at last in the turbid water, not three feet deep, I saw swift streaks darting from a mass that was obviously fluid yet seemed solid, and then darting back again. '*Chopé. Chopé. Chopé.*' A barracuda pressed towards the seething curve the shrunken sphere the devil had now become. But long before he reached it he stopped dead as though he had struck an impassable sound-barrier. Terror swept back hundreds of fish, a mixed multitude jostled together by fright, species mingled in panic-stricken hordes.

Now it was the women alone who held the mass of swarming creatures. One by one the men had left the pocket as it grew smaller and smaller and fetched the spears which had been stuck upright in the sand of the breach. Alphonse climbed down from his look-out post. He had completely lost his voice but he ran to take part in the final phase.

Blue and black carangues,[1] red or silver snappers with spatulate mouths, mérous[2] spotted purple, mérous spotted red with purple rings, parrot-fish of all sorts, dawas, surgeon-fish, file-fish, barracudas, globe-fish, sea-hedgehogs and many others . . . the largest the first victims. A great blue-green parrot-fish with its belly ripped open was thrashing the sand. A ray wriggled round the iron that nailed it to the ground. An amber snapper—maybe since his death blow he had changed colour—dragged the tapping haft of a spear right on to the sand. Some fish stranded and were at once seized by the gills and flung higher up on the beach.

Chop-Chop, the old mongrel, showing his teeth and growling, seized an enormous file-fish by the head, trying to pull it along as he swam. With a powerful movement the fish

---

(1) Carangues are fish of the *Carangidae* family, some of which are known in English as 'horse-mackerel'. (2) Mérous are fish of the genus *Serranus*, 'rock-cod'.

wrenched itself free. Then the dog, snarling with fury, leapt forward. His head disappeared in the bloody water, but you could follow the struggle by watching the angry jerks of the dog's back above the surface. Then Chop-Chop pulled out the lifeless file-fish.

One old woman could not dodge the tail-lash of a huge dawa. She let it slip from her arms and sucked blood from her right hand, ripped open by the dreadful horned spur. She tore the tattered hem off her dress to make a dressing.

By now the devil was a thin crescent of water close inshore, violently heaving and churning. The panic-stricken fish struggled about in a bloody pool now too shallow to cover them. Their slamming, slapping bodies raised a deafening uproar. Bits of fish flew about everywhere, whipping the faces and blinding the eyes of the men as they stepped back to hurl their harpoons. When there were no longer any big fish the remainder were left to the children, and they eagerly grabbed the weapons offered to them by their elders.

Chop-Chop, plastered with sand and smeared with guts and scales, was watching closely the interminable triple line of fish laid out on the burning sand. They were still showing some signs of life. A carangue arched in one last effort. The dog ran up barking and stood with ears pricked before the shuddering body. The carangue died, and as it died it changed colour. Chop-Chop sniffed at it, backed away, and then turned to watch a blue méron still flopping about twenty yards or so away.

The women had lighted a fire of dry coconut fibre and palm-leaves. They waddled and wriggled beside the red flames and the dresses clinging to their bodies quickly dried out. Their chattering teeth were due as much to playfulness as to more than two hours immersion in cold water.

Alphonse presided over the share-out. First of all he pointed to the chief's fish and two young lads with rippling muscles picked them up and placed them at Pierre Dumai's feet.

Pierre, with a smile of pride and satisfaction, raised the fish a little in my direction. After all it was true that this fishing had been held in my honour. I did not know what to say or what to do, so I just admired the offerings in silence. They consisted of a quite remarkably large carangue and an even larger barracuda.

On the sand lay the great net, used once and discarded.

19 The Big Bugna

'THERE, that's for you! And that! And that!'

The women sitting in the shade began to giggle when old Léocadie started slashing with a matchet at an enormous pumpkin. She kept up her mocking laughter as she raised her skinny arm and shouted curses in the Mouli language. From the laughter, the expressions, the chuckles of the gossips gathered together to prepare for the great festival, it was clear that the men of the tribe were getting what was coming to them in the way of sarcasm and derision. And from some of their looks I gathered I was included with the rest.

Ignace's wife, who was leaning against the papaw-tree, grabbed by his neck a big bronze cock that was next to the string of hens lying on the mat. She held the bird tight between her stout thighs and squeezed him with her left hand, while with her right she pulled out one of the long tail-feathers and felt for a place to drive in its point. She found what she was looking for at the joint between two bones and gave a slight jab. The cock's eyes opened wide, then closed, and his head dropped. Then this powerful woman untied the legs of the dead creature and stretched out her hand toward the hens that were cackling from fright and struggling in vain to scramble to their feet.

The girls came back from the plantations. Their foreheads were covered with beads of sweat and their soaking clothes clung to their bodies. They put down the yams, taros, and sweet potatoes still powdered with dry earth. Old women, in faded clothes, began to peel them with rusty razor blades and broken bottle-ends. When Léocadie had handed out her bits of pumpkin, she came and helped pluck the dead chickens.

In a broken, raucous voice she burst into song, which was taken up in chorus by the other women. Some of them were using their nails to scale fish brought in from the devil the day before and kept in a shady place. Others were splitting coconuts and grating the flesh into pulp in enamel bowls. Great banana leaves, like some supple plastic material of a delicate green, were spread on darker green palm-leaves that covered the ground. These waterproof plant mats were first of all decorated with vegetables and on this bed other food was placed: here a blue-green parrot-fish, with a brown-spotted méron and a tiny butterfly-fish, yellow with a black tuft and quite stiff, for it still had its delicate scales, then there would be two pieces of a large carangue sticking out too far—the head (thrown to the quarrelling dogs) and the tail had to be sliced off, elsewhere lay chickens, joints of pork, a sucking pig or a goat. All this was plentifully sprinkled with coconut milk. The fatty liquid was squeezed out, as if trickling from two brown millstones, by the knotted hands of a very old and very thin woman who was most careful to scatter the milk properly. She plunged her hands into the flocky, thick pulp in the big bowl enamelled with flowers, and lifted and pressed the dazzling white mass, and when she had finished there remained nothing but an absolutely dry residue.

When it had been thus moistened, the food was wrapped carefully, first in one thickness of banana-leaves, then in another, and then in a third before the palm-leaves were knotted underneath to produce a hermetically sealed sack of verdure. About forty of these bulky sacks were carried off to the mounds which had been raised among the few clumps of coco-palms on the beach. The sacks were placed on a bed of white-hot stones and then covered with all the old iron the tribe possessed. Broken lids, smashed chains, bits of cast-iron pots, sheet-metal, useless tools—all became red-hot. On top they threw old sacks, and then sand was heaped over everything.

Through the hubbub of stifled cries, excited calls and songs, and all the joyful, light-hearted restlessness which had run through the whole tribe since daybreak, came the discordant notes of a guitar being tuned. Suddenly there was a violent broadside of shouting and argument. What could be happening? A quarrel, a fight?

'It's nothing,' said one of the young women with a smile, as she heaped sand on one of the mounds. 'It's the men playing cards.'

A friend who came back from the USA some years ago told me this—it could be true, or it could be the product of his lively imagination:

There was in New York a club, with a membership of business-men and politicians who would meet after office hours in a jungle setting. The cloakroom lockers contained the weapons and clothing of primitive tribesmen (animal skins, costumes of African warriors, leg coverings and mocassins of Sioux or Apaches), which these gentlemen, for the most part at least middle-aged, would put on. At the same time they assumed a new personality. To rid themselves of the murderous desires they had stifled during the day, these gentlemen shouted invectives at each other, swore hatred and contempt at one another, threatened each other with clubs, spears and toma-hawks, challenged one another with horrifying, appalling grimaces . . . and after that, they felt relieved and would go off to the bar arm in arm, roaring with laughter at the most dreadful tortures they had been imagining a few minutes before. And so they prepared themselves for still another day of civilized life.

Decorated with ribbons, and with their faces made up, Néophyte, Victor, Benoît, Julien and Alphonse sat together on a mat, slamming down the cards so violently that corners already dog-eared shot across the floor. It was rather like a game of tarot. No stakes, no money was involved. But if the whole future of the tribe had depended on it, I do not think these men could have betrayed more ill-temper. They held their cards as though they were weapons, and hurled them as though they were bombs, shouting insults and unintelligible imprecations. Where in this furious being was the usually imperturbable Benoît? I could hardly recognize the good-humoured, chaffing Alphonse in that fat man, with a face convulsed with fury. What had become of Néophyte's modesty? He was bawling louder than his pig when they had killed it that morning. And Julien's reticence? Even Victor's stammer had disappeared! The fraternity of these men demanded by Custom must require a certain amount of unconscious effort and the strain of this is relaxed in card games. For the fertile invention of invective you would have to look a long way to equal Victor's calling Néophyte, I think it was, a shark with two cocks, and no use for either . . .

Iviki came running to tell the players that Pierre Dumai invited them to the Big House, for the time had come to gather together for the banquet. They got up smiling and followed the child, chatting pleasantly together.

Garlands of palm-leaves were hung up wherever possible, like growing leaves. The Big House had quickly taken on a festive look. On the short grass armfuls of great, shining leaves from the banana-grove near the courtyard had been laid down side by side, making a huge delicate-green carpet far morei charmng and beautiful than any embroidered or damask tablecloth ever spread upon a banquet table. Men, women, children and old people, all beribboned and in their Sunday best, many of them with their faces painted in bright colours—each prepared his place at table. They cut a little sharp-edged spoon from a filao branch, for sticking in to the meat and fish; from half a palm-leaf they deftly plaited a sort of pretty, concave vessel lined with a taro leaf. Pyramids of green balls had been piled up—coconuts, properly unripe and well filled with liquid. One arranged everything in front of one before sitting down. Pierre put me beside him—in our place of honour. Then he sat still and bowed his head in a reverential attitude, and the two hundred and fifty diners became silent. 'O Lord, bless us and bless this meal of which we are about to partake. Give bread to those who have none. Amen.' And the chorus of guests echoed 'Amen', as they made the sign of the cross. Then they sat down. A very young girl came to crown me with flowers and, from shyness no doubt, she embraced me so abruptly that our lips touched.

'Bravo. Good shot. Encore. Encore.'

The poor child was so shy that she remained bending over me and kept her hand on her lips, while from one end to the other of the great greensward came cries of encouragement for us to start again.

A little orchestra of string instruments struck up to accompany the singers, who were some distance away. I recognized the tune Guy had been trying out some time before when he was tuning his guitar. The touchingly simple melody was the tribal hymn, and all around began to sing it softly. The two guitarists and the ukulele player were accompanied by a double-bass—a cord tied to the handle of an oil-can and a whittled down tree-branch that served as the neck. The plater modulated the pitch with his big toe.

Shouts of joy and murmurs of satisfaction greeted the arrival of the courses. Green, red, blue, white, orange, violet, golden yellow, purple . . . the light muslin of Mission dresses fluttered in the breeze and flashed in the sunlight, as the women brought the smoking bugnas they had just dug up from the beach. One of the women came and placed the first of the sacks before Pierre Dumai and me. Then she opened it. The outside palm-leaves were quite charred, but inside their moisture had kept the leaves green, and they gave a delicious flavour to the fish they enveloped.

I committed a double imprudence. I allowed Pierre Dumai to help me and then, what was worse, I did honour to the generous helping he piled in front of me. Then I realized that he and I had to taste every dish, every bugna! And Pierre was much more attentive to my feasting than to his own. No doubt he must see that the chief guest should not escape eating as much as he possibly could. After the fourth or fifth of these containers that opened like great flowers, each containing some new dish, I was completely satisfied. But other dishes kept on being put before us. My small plant bowl was already filled with gristle and bones—and the banquet had only just begun. I just could not eat any more. But how could I upset my friends? And how they could eat! Alphonse guzzled assiduously and from time to time wiped his fingers on his pandanus garlands. He reminded me of some truculent Indian chief[1] come back from a distant cruise, feasting riotously at a country fair. Skinny and dried up as she was, old Léocadie opposite me ate as much if not more than her neighbours. Her movements were methodical, deliberate, and her wrinkled face and chin were daubed with sauce. At least she did lose her rather solemn air. On my right was Iviki, no longer the charming child who on the day of my arrival had gazed up at me with wide eyes. His belly was now inflated like a balloon. He frowned as he hastily devoured an enormous fish, from which he did not take his eyes except to stare covetously at the fresh bugnas which kept on being opened.

Pierre Dumai would not listen to my protests—he thought, no doubt, that they were just conventional expressions of politeness. So he overwhelmed me with encouragements to eat more and more.

Now came the coconut crabs. The largest was set down before me.

---

(1) Morenhout—*Voyages en Oceanie*—'Through my spy-glass I saw Indians wearing neither hats nor stockings.'

'Pierre, have a heart!'

He burst out laughing. 'I'd pity you if you'd nothing to eat.'

He burst the ventral pocket of a crab over my bowl and released a mass of golden-yellow fat with a strong odour of copra.

'Taste the yellow part. It's better than anything.'

I had to admit it really was delicious. After all, despite the creature's monstrous appearance, it was only a crab. But how could I get down more than a few mouthfuls? I was saved by the first of the floor-shows . . .

'Race for children walking on their hands,' shouted Génio, and he waved a red *paräu* ready for the start.

They were children from the banquet and they were going to walk on their hands! They jostled together in a row, with their hands on the ground and one leg in the air, watching for the cloth.

'Ready. One, two, three, go.' Génio lowered his *paräu*. Off they went amid laughter and cheers. Not one of them appeared to be the slightest bit upset at playing this game, the very sight of which made me feel sick. I felt so ill I shut my eyes, and only opened them when the cheers had died down.

'Sack-race for women.'

About ten women got up from the banquet and slipped into old copra sacks. Most of them were so shaking with laughter that they could not hold the edges as high as their breasts. And in spite of my discomfort, I began laughing. The others were crazy with delight. Old Sophie had outdistanced her rivals from the start, but she stumbled, and fat Noémi could not avoid her and fell on the top of her. While they were tangled a girl bobbed past them like a grasshopper and was well on her way to the winning post. But she too tripped and fell, and others fell over her, so that it was the prudent Joséphine who won, though she had so far been easily last.

'Sack-race for girls,' shouted Génio, after the women had

gone back to their places and had started eating again. Then came the turn of the men to show their skill. 'Nut stripping competition.' Before each competitor were placed three coconuts, and beside them a stake pointed at both ends. At the signal, each man stuck his stake in the ground, and with the stake he had to strip the skin from the nuts. No nut must be pierced—the slightest seepage of its liquid meant disqualification—nor must the judge be shown a nut with the slightest trace of fibre: the surface must be absolutely smooth. The most skilled at this common task can scale a nut in five traditional movements.

'Ready. One, two, three, go.'

Génio dropped his *parāu*.

The competitors were lined up. Néophyte started rapidly, and so did Guy. With a powerful lateral twist, Benoît managed to reduce the traditional movements to four. It was fascinating to watch the action of his strong, broad, efficient hands. Néophyte held out his third and last nut at the very moment that Benoît beat Guy by a tenth of a second. Génio examined the last nut and handed it back to Néophyte.

'Disqualified.'

'What?' Néophyte's face fell. 'Why? I've won!'

'Not on your life. I saw a drop when you struck.'

'You're daft. What drop?'

'A drop, a drop. You bashed too hard. I'm the judge, remember that. I saw it.'

'Coconut milk in your eye . . .'

Génio put the nut to his lips, sucked and spat out a little liquid as proof.

'That's not from the nut. You're spitting.'

Génio once more put his mouth to the nut and sucked hard and long. This time everyone could see he spat what was definitely a spurt of clear coconut milk.

'Benoît first, Guy second, Alphonse third. Néophyte disqualified.'

Génio's decision was final. Néophyte protested, but he calmed down little by little and took his place at the banquet again.

'Make-up competition.'

There was a committee to judge which girl had devised the most original creation, in the best taste. I noticed in some of the 'paintings' a geometric sense similar to that I had seen displayed in the tapas at Wallis, but here pictures were embellished by a touch of poetical imagination—suns, moons at different phases, stars and comets. These astral designs evoked the saga of the forefathers guided by stars to what was to become their homeland.

The judges could not come to a decision, so Pierre Dumai asked me to choose between the two finalists. The girls were very excited. They held one another's hands with fingers interlaced, and fixed on me brown, brilliant eyes full of hope and apprehension.

One of the picture-faces depicted the calm immensity of the sea under a night sky pierced with stars. The other represented the birth of a floral world. What a pity that in a few hours these paintings would be washed away!

Impossible to decide. Each was as beautiful as the other.

The pictorial faces were distorted by broad smiles as my suggestion was adopted that they should both be classed together *ex aequo* as the winners.

Now it was the turn of the old women. They had to sit and plait baskets from long palm-leaves beside them. 'Ready,' warned Génio. 'One, two, three, go.' With calm, almost mechanical movements of their hands, like tools, and with astonishing speed, they built up an area of interlaced strands. I think the slowest competitor took less than three minutes to finish her basket before going to join the others at the banquet—still going strong.

Now from behind the Big House came the women's orchestra, followed by the dancers. Musicians beat the ground with resounding drums—thick bamboos cut into different lengths—and whistling with their fingers in their mouths like hooligans or with thumb and forefinger. The musicians beat on bottles and tins, and clapped their hands.

I can remember white dresses, and faces daubed with sand and blue chalk, dancers hissing a rhythm through their teeths . . . and then everything jumbled and faded into the far, far distance. I had the feeling my head was swinging to and fro, and voices nearby penetrated in waves my woolly calm, slipping into unconsciousness. And I seemed to be falling, falling . . . I was too surprised to be frightened. Then I felt a great bump which revived me and half-stunned me at the same time. A canopy of light sparkled above me. I was under water. I was swallowing it. I was stifling. At last I got to the air. The sea was breaking against the foot of the cliff. From above many voices called out:

'Bravo, bravo. Are you all right? Can you swim? Bravo. Bravo. Go on, swim. Go on.'

Everything was all right, though I was still confused like when you pass out from shock, and can remember doing so, but not what caused it. My legs were rather wobbly, but I managed to set foot on the sand and I was soon surrounded by people expressing the most friendly solicitude. 'Better now? Not sick any more? Does you good, eh? We knew you'd be all right.' Only then did I realize that these curious friends had without further ado pitched me into the sea from the top of the cliff. What had happened for me to be treated like that? A mixture of indigestion and sunstroke? It did not matter, but I didn't hide my ill-temper.

'And what if I'd drowned?'

'Of course we'd never have let you drown,' declared Génio. He seemed eager to convince me that such desertion would have been quite impossible. 'We'd have jumped in too. We wouldn't have left you on the bottom to drown.'

Yes, no doubt, I was making myself ridiculous. An old

skin-diver does not drown as quickly as that. And the men around me were reliable men. They were not only convinced they had done well in not hesitating to apply to me the treatment Custom dictates in the circumstances, but they were very pleased to see I was in good shape. That was, in fact, quite true. I felt well, really very well, in spite of the heavy weight in my stomach. In France I would have spent at least twenty-four hours in bed. The shock, the sudden, enormous difference in surroundings, in temperature? Instinct aroused and injected into the body some secret store of energy sufficient to counter-balance and dissipate the effects of the organism's failure? Why not? The frontiers of medical knowledge are constantly being bombarded by the revelations of empirical evidence. At least it's worthy of discussion.

Suddenly I started to laugh. The idea of a man sick from too much good food being tipped into the sea was highly comic. And after all, I had not shown up so badly. I was beginning to feel rather proud of myself, partly for having survived such prehistoric medical treatment, and also because I was experiencing its excellent effects.

Which all goes to show there are some things which cannot be treated—vanity among them.

'men themselves become Sea Eagles'
overleaf: 'before I saw the fish catch the light, Mathias was already in the air'

20 *Thalassotherapy*

THE next day I woke up as though nothing had happened. Perhaps I was beginning to get adapted to the Mouli way of life. I felt full of energy and appetite as I made my way to the Big House, where my breakfast was waiting for me. Génio, while still talking to Pierre Dumai, looked me over closely.

'How are you?'

'Fine, Génio, thanks.'

'You're not angry with us for throwing you in the sea? You know . . .'

'Not at all,' I cut in. 'On the contrary, it did me good.'

'You'd eaten too much bugna,' said Pierre, smiling.

'That was your fault. But I must admit it was very good.'

Pierre was pleased by the compliment and bowed slightly. But Génio had to go on with his explanations.

'We saw you'd passed out. You looked like a corpse. In cases like that the medicine of the Ancients recommends us to throw the sick man into the sea. We tried to stand you upright, but no good, you fell and didn't move. But in the sea it's different. You have to swim, and if you swim it's all right, you're cured.'

'Of course, Génio. I'm very satisfied, believe me, and very grateful. I'll tell my grandchildren how you looked after me. Better than the best doctor.'

A smile of relief passed over Génio's face.

'The sea's wonderful medicine,' I went on. 'One never feels so well as after a few hours under water.'

'That's true.' Pierre took me seriously. 'The Ancients also said that those who want to keep young should often go into the sea. When an old man stays a long time in the water, his

'Néophyte reappeared triumphant, with a magnificent parrot-fish skewered on his trident'

'it was a female blue shark. Benoît's blow had struck the spine and killed it at once' skin and muscles become firm like a young lad. Maybe he's a little tired, but after a good rest he'll be stronger than before.'

Well, one had only to think of their appearance to be convinced of it. Every one of the Elders seemed healthy and vigorous. The youthfulness of Mathias especially was little short of phenomenal.

'Not only stay in the water,' went on Pierre, 'but drink it'.

'Drink sea-water?'

'Of course.'

'Very much?'

'Oh, twenty-five or thirty pints. More.'

'What? Drink twenty-five pints of sea-water?'

'That's our way of cleaning ourselves out, our aperient . . .'

'But Pierre, a man would die if he drank as much as that!'

'Not on your life,' put in Génio. 'Once a year all men over fifty have a day when they go and drink sea-water from morning to evening. And afterwards, mark my words, like young fellows'—he made a gesture with his arm—'and if the old woman of an old man who's had his sea-water treatment isn't too old, there you are—a baby!'

I was dumbfounded. Who in my place would not have been, including my friend Alain Bombard?

A few days later I was able to check the truth of what Génio had said, though maybe Mathias during his day of purification did not swallow quite twenty-five pints.

'The old man eats nothing in the morning before going into the sea. He begins to drink the water with the juice of certain herbs that he crushes between his hands. The more he drinks the better it is for him. The water comes out everywhere and his whole body is well cleaned, just like new again. Sometimes after nine or ten pints the old man gets tired of drinking. Then he stands for a while without moving, but afterwards he must go on. When the sun sinks—finished. The old man goes back to his hut, drinks a bowl of well-sugared tea and sleeps all night under a blanket. The next morning, there he is, younger than a young man. And he stays young for months, never gets tired or sick.'

From dawn to dusk drinking sea-water . . .

'Aren't there ever any accidents?'

'Once an old man died,' Pierre admitted, 'but his heart had been weak a long time and maybe he would soon have died even if he had not drunk the water. It's better to obey Custom and take a sea-water treatment every year than to fear death. If one must die, one dies.'

So it was their observance of this ritual rule of Customary medicine that gave the men a vigour that would astonish all the Fausts of the earth, did they but know of it. After all, it can be applied everywhere. Perhaps this treatment is only the beginning of a new science called 'Thalassotherapy'.[1]

Could not the serum of youth, as at Mouli, just be taken in cupped hands dipped in the most inexhaustible of all elixirs?

Travel Notes I was wrong in rather dreading the arrival of the priest who stays at Mouli every other fortnight. How would he welcome the presence among his flock of a stranger in the prime of life? Would I not seem to him simply a disturber of the peace, who ought to be expelled? The Pacific reeks with stories of religious intolerance and if anyone was vulnerable, surely I was.

But things went off very well. The young priest came on foot from the Fayawa passage (three miles along the beach in terrific heat; his cassock was drenched in sweat) and proved very broadminded. He listened to my story with sympathy, even interest. We dined together at the presbytery (I brought with me some fish harpooned in the Wassaü passage) which, like the church, was built at the time when the population was being converted. Both buildings bore

---

(1) From *thalassa*, sea, and *therapeuein*, to treat.

the marks of their age—thick, irregular walls washed white with coral lime—an austerity which marked a dividing line between simplicity and poverty.

We talked about religion. I declared beliefs. 'In fact you're a pantheist.' I admitted it. I said that conversion to Christianity had been possible because the missionaries in the middle of the last century brought with them a message that differed in form only, and not in principle, from the natives' own belief in a superior divine being. And Christian morality was in many respects the same as that imposed by Custom, and this must have greatly impressed the people of Mouli. Religion hereabouts has a quality of great charm and one would have to be insincere not to acknowledge that. But I will keep to my own 'adogmatism'.

At that expression the young priest smiled. As we parted, I said how pleased I was that he did not consider me a fiend worthy of his malediction. He smiled again. 'You are only a traveller.' That touched me on the raw. It was something I had banished to an indefinite future. But it's true. I am only a traveller.

21 Pavlov's Pig

WE all know about Pavlov's famous experiments which, by making dogs' mouths water, revealed the existence of conditioned reflexes. My mind is rather parochial, and not altogether free from pedantry, but Sophie, Mathias's wife, proved to me by practical demonstration, that the famous conditioned reflexes were known at Mouli—in fact that knowledge of them had been handed down as part of the wisdom of their ancestors. With all deference to the memory of Pavlov, I think I am well fitted to show how this science is employed.

I had been very surprised to see that one old woman, as she walked about from hut to hut, was always accompanied by a faithful little pig. It had the classic corkscrew tail and displayed such affectionate obedience, such an eagerness to please and such touching familiarity that many of our Western owners of pedigree dogs would have been green with envy if they had seen him. I did know that among some primitive tribes, for instance in New Guinea, women will suckle piglets at the same time as their own baby—one breast for each: a tropical version of Romulus and Remus. But on reflection it seems less surprising than what goes on at Mouli. After all, disciplined behaviour, obedience and a display of attachment to a man or woman, are all things quite incompatible with the usual character of the porcine race. At Mouli I was told that it was quite a usual thing to make a pig 'gentle'. Moreover Sophie would be undertaking this operation in a few days' time. So I went off to see the smiling Sophie and she promised not to set to work without letting me know.

On the appointed day Sophie cut a few taro leaves, picked

up an old jute sack and led me towards an enclosure of wattled palm trunks inside which was a grunting sow and several newly weaned piglets. There were terrible screams when Sophie grabbed one of the young creatures, but the sow calmly chewed on the taro leaves Sophie had thrown to her. Sophie bundled the piglet into the sack, tied it with a liana, threw the squeaking and wriggling mass over her shoulder and went off quietly to put it down in a little copra shed.

I was agog to find out what was going to happen now.

'Finished,' said Sophie.

'You're going to leave him like that?'

'Till tomorrow morning.'

'Don't forget to send for me.'

The next morning Sophie half freed a piglet crazy with fury. She managed to hold on tight (its belly and hind legs were still in the sack) as he made a mad rush toward the light. Then she offered him little bits of copra she had cut up specially. His cries nearly deafened me. But the little pig was so hungry that his cries were gradually interrupted by grunts, half of anger and half of satisfaction, and he gobbled up his copra greedily. Then Sophie shoved him back in the sack.

'Finished.'

'Until when?'

'Once at midday, once in the evening.'

Twice during this first day and thereafter three times, the piglet popped out of his prison like a jack-in-the-box, yelling and struggling with all his might, and Sophie, calm and smiling, held him in her arms and managed to make him take his meal of leaves and copra. On the third day I noticed a marked change. When the liana was unloosened and his snout appeared in the light, he stretched out *at once* to the food, and he ate it—still grunting, it is true, but he restrained his frenzied anger until Sophie pushed him gently but ruthlessly into the dark sack again and left him there.

There was no doubt the animal had been conditioned to

associate the handling of the sack with the absorption of food. So much so that when he was released for the third time on the fifth day, the piglet welcomed the bits of copra with little cries of satisfaction and remained quietly in the sack while taking his meals. He even allowed himself to be patted and stroked. Sophie's hands were his foster-mother's.

As we were walking back to our huts Sophie said, 'It's all right now. Tomorrow he'll come out a bit.'

The first chapter of the education appeared to be finished. But what a hysterical crisis when, after she had fed him and let him out of the sack, Sophie knotted a strong liana round his belly and led him on a leash. I realized the most difficult part was to come. The greatest patience was necessary before the refractory piglet was again conditioned, this time to identify his moments of liberty on the leash with complete obedience to Sophie. The delight of stretching his legs on the warm sand came to an end at the moment he showed any signs of disobedience—then back he went into the sack. Some days passed by, with ups and downs. Sophie told me in confidence that we were up against a pig with lots of character and that most likely it would be a week before the final test. Opening of the sack: food: walk. Opening of the sack: food: walk. Opening of the sack: food: walk.

For a time I ceased to attend every performance. Then, one morning, Iviki called me from outside my hut. I slipped on a *parāu* and stepped briskly into the open. It was early in the morning. Why were all the kids headed for the beach? Sophie was inviting me to watch her little pig set quite free for the first time.

Sophie had the young animal on the leash. They were walking on the sands. She held out to him a piece of copra and he munched it with delight. Then she took him in her arms and fondled him for some time. Then finally she undid the liana and put the freed piglet down. He did not lose a moment. He made off at top speed straight ahead right away from his mistress. She called after him in vain. What he did not know, however, was that from the start the children had encircled him. All his tricks were thwarted and at last he was flattened on the ground, squealing as loud as on the first days. This boarder was (for his own good) spending most of his life in a dungeon. How was it all going to end? Maybe he was one of those untamable specimens and perhaps poor Sophie was getting attached in vain to a creature she would never break in. She did not answer my questions. I did not insist because her usual smile seemed just a little forced.

I was coming back from some fishing one day when I met my Sophie on the beach; she whistled through her teeth at the little pig who was rolling about delightedly in the warm sand, without a leash at all. He at once jumped up to join her and rubbed his back against her legs. I congratulated her. This time one could read satisfaction and pride in her smile. She had been well rewarded for all her trouble. The charming little pig trotted along by her side as they made their way to her hut. He had recognized her as mistress.

Now I have a tale to tell when I hear Pavlov quoted.

22 *Crawfish*[1]

Extract from *La France Australe* (a New Caledonia daily published at Nouméa) of 1956: 'Since yesterday a stuffed "china" crawfish, slightly over six feet long (antennae included) and weighing about twenty-seven pounds, has been on show in Balande's shop-window.'

IN the hands of thriller writers the most ordinary thing may become invested with manic terror. Think of what Hitchcock can do just with a creaking door. Since Daphne Du Maurier's *The Birds* it seems possible that, in some horrible way, the advent of the harbingers of spring may represent dreadful danger. I know a young mother who finished reading this story sitting in a public garden. Suddenly she jumped up and seized her little boy in her arms—he had been playing near a flock of pigeons.

I think anyone who had listened to the story Benoît told me as he steered his little boat back to Mouli would have been unable to see a crawfish when he dived under water without shuddering.

The giant crawfish stones were about four fathoms down on the bed of the lagoon, a short way from the Fayawa passage.

'In an hour, if this wind holds,' said Benoît as we were getting into the dinghy.

Guy handed me the underwater fishing gear and Néophyte passed me a demijohn of fresh water. Then they got on board and we steered for Fayawa.

They had known the place for a long time. Benoît had taken

---

(1) Crawfish: that is, the rock, or spiny, lobster (*langouste* in French).

his bearings on an *amer*—a coco-palm of a peculiar shape—on the shore three or four hundred yards away. Néophyte hauled down the sail and Guy quickly dropped the anchor.

I leaned over the gunwhale: 'Is this the place?'

My tone of voice must have shown I was disappointed. Benoît looked at me: 'Something wrong?'

'You can't see anything.'

'It's clear at the bottom.' He put on his diving goggles.

Not being able to see in tropical waters is something that I shall never be able to get used to. The water is not often transparent in the lagoons because their bottom consists of almost weightless coral dust some of which remains in suspension. But I had rarely seen water so turbid as this was. My companions dived overboard. Willy-nilly I had to do the same. I could hardly see the weapon I was holding. The other men had at once disappeared in a green opacity. I made my way down apprehensively, a blind man in a fluid.

At last I could distinguish the blurred outlines of bodies against the bulbous madrepores gashed with cracks and riddled with grottoes. Guy was aiming between the antennae of a giant crawfish. So large was the target that it seemed incongruous he should aim at all . . . then suddenly I forgot my discomfort in the most violent anguish I have ever felt. What I took at first to be a moray eel of some huge, unknown sort pounced on to me. We faced one another, both of us upright. The creature's undulating length was balanced on its spatulate tail. From the triangular, bulging head, quite close to mine, tiny eyes were staring at me. It must be the great serpent that I had always dreaded meeting. Its bite is immediately fatal. The creature moved away a little. The interminable blackish body was undulating with sinister grace . . . then it disappeared.

Guy surfaced. His crawfish was flapping violently. The harpoon on which it was impaled had bent over at right angles. We were now in the air once more.

'Guy,' I panted, 'get out of the water, quick. There's a horribly dangerous serpent.'

'Harmless.'

He was fully occupied in struggling with his refractory prize and he paid no more attention to me.

Perhaps nothing is more contagious than fear, but nothing can more effectively combat it than the fear of showing it to those who do not share it. I suddenly remembered that plate in a book on ichthyology: *marine serpents*, a cut from their fangs . . . fatal. These men here had not read that book. They had just seen the creatures did not attack human beings.

'Harmless,' Néophyte also said as he came up, dragging with difficulty a 'china' crawfish. 'You always see four or five serpents around about the stones. But they never bite.'

He turned over the crawfish that was clutching the bottom of the boat and with its tail, as broad as two hands, thrashing the planks. Néophyte took a deep breath and dived in again, I behind the white soles of his feet as they vanished rapidly in the greenish, opaque water. Two long, serpentine forms emerged from nowhere and glided towards me, guardians of marine catacombs against our intrusion. The icy inspection of their glassy eyes. My companions were behaving as though the reptiles did not exist. The crawfish which at last I managed to find on the bottom, twisted my harpoon like a hair-pin, but I did get it to the surface and threw it in the boat. Then, having preserved my reputation, I stayed up above in the universe of light. Sunny, familiar.

We would have to tack to reach Mouli. Benoît were about to get the wind. The sail flapped for a few minutes fore and aft, then it bellied and swung to starboard. Néophyte made fast the sheet. The little craft bobbed about and gathered speed.

Our prizes were astonishingly lively. The smallest of them, bashing its tail on the planking, was three times as big as a craw-fish of normal size. How much would the largest one weigh?

'Thirteen pounds, maybe fourteen or fifteen,' suggested Néophyte.

'Have you ever seen a larger?' I asked.

'Not often.'

'There was a crawfish over six feet long shown at Nouméa, six feet long and maybe twenty-five pounds. That must have been a monster. There can't be any bigger than that.'

'Oh, yes, there are bigger ones,' said Benoît.

'You've seen them?'

Guy and Néophyte met Benoît's eyes.

'No one on Mouli. It was a Leikigné man who told the story. A crawfish thicker than a coco-palm trunk, not a small palm, a big one. It ate his pal.'

This is Benoît's story:

'Two men of the Leikigné tribe went to dive down on to the stones where the "china" crawfish are. One went down and did not come up. The other was some way away. Minutes went by before he realized he was alone. He began to get anxious. The water was very thick and disturbed. He dived down many times but could see nothing. Nothing on the surface either. He dived again. At last on the bottom he saw two legs sticking out of a hole. He went near. The body was being dragged along by this gigantic crawfish. He was out of breath and he had to surface. Then he summoned all his courage and dived in again. The feet were now under the stone. Then they disappeared. When this man got back to his tribe his face was as grey as ashes. For some days his eyes stared like a madman.'

Benoît assumed the expression of a man whose eyes were bulging from their sockets with terror.

'They found the body?'

'Never on your life, no, nothing.'

'It's impossible. The man who told that story must have been crazy!'

'One of the old men of the Leikigné said that too,' put in

Néophyte. 'He said the other man had been drowned or seized by a shark. But no one listened to him. The man who died swam like a dolphin. Certainly he wasn't drowned. And no man, dead or alive, was ever carried off by a shark in the lagoon.'

'Did anyone ever see the crawfish again?'

'Some very large crawfish have been sighted, but none as thick though as a palm-trunk.'

'It must have disappeared?'

'Maybe it came up from the very bottom of the lagoon,' said Néophyte.

'The grandfather or the grandmother of all crawfish,' Guy roared out laughing. 'It nabbed a Leikigné man. If it had been a Mouli man, it would have been the crawfish that would have got eaten.'

Guy was only about ten years old at the time. The story terrified the Leikigné and Mouli tribes, whose territories, as we have seen, are separated only by the Fayawa passage. For Guy the tale was like the legends told by the Elders, who themselves got their tales from old dodderers still living who claim to have seen the devil, even to have spoken to him. For Benoît and Néophyte the thing had actually happened as the man of Leikigné had described it. As a matter of fact, anything could come out of the sea. We know almost nothing about it.

Note Although this story was confirmed by several of the Elders of Mouli, I could not believe it. It did induce me, though, to seek information later about a race of giant and possibly anthropophagous crustaceans. I came across an Australian publication containing the description of the capture of a 'china' crawfish weighing thirty-six pounds and about seven feet long. The creature was taken by aboriginals in a small island of the Coral Sea. There was no photograph.

23 A Sociologist in Mouli

MODERN sociologists think that the true value of a country's culture is to be judged by the comparative social status of women with men. The greater the influence of women the higher the level of civilization. In a few decades, maybe even before, women sociologists using this criterion—which I believe is Anglo-American—will be trying to find out how far the position of men is causing a decline in matriarchal civilization.

In my opinion, as regards the relative position of men and women, society on Mouli offers the example of a civilization which maintains about the best possible balance between the natural antagonisms of the two contrasting sexes. Taken as a whole, or singly, the women offer an astonishing and very rare spectacle; although they only make reasonable use of their liberty, they seem happy and satisfied. I tried in vain to discover the secret of this exemplary state of things. The men were uncommunicative.

All I got was a mysterious (or final: one can take one's choice) pronouncement from Ignace. 'Men are men, women are women.' The other Elders nodded their heads, but the conversation went no farther. If, however, I were a sociologist entrusted with the task of drawing up a report on the tribal intercourse of the Mouli people, this is what my account would be (it being of course understood that I may be mistaken, since it is the speciality of specialists to be deceived):

The harmony existing between the men and women of this tribe appears to be derived from a very fortunate compatibility between the temperaments of most individuals and also, more especially, to the observance of the Customary principles which condition social life. The people of Mouli attach great importance to marriage—and in a wider sense to betrothals—for this institution represents the non-political structure of their society, and without it that society would collapse. The realization of this not only derives from the Customary principles but is no doubt one of the most significant of them. Every individual who directly or indirectly disturbs the harmony reigning between a married couple would then be attacking the fundamental basis of society. He would be acting in full knowledge of what he was doing and in full realization of the hostility he would excite against himself.

From the very first, children are brought up in complete freedom, but it is a freedom which does not preclude unlimited respect for parents, and this respect is the first of all the precepts of Custom. Kindness, and feelings of friendship and gratitude are developed by the habit, formed very early on, of sharing with others and of making one another small presents. No hypocrisy is shown in withholding from children knowledge of sexual matters. They are explained in all simplicity to the young as soon as they get inquisitive about them. Indecency is unknown, because there are no inhibitions. Daily life is lived in such a way that few acts can remain secret. The real character of each man and woman is known to all. Before a man and woman become definitely engaged to be married they know quite well what they are doing. The equitable division of belongings cuts at the very root of any pecuniary consideration. Young men and women therefore simply follow their personal feelings without material considerations.

The young man, dressed in his best clothes, will go and make his request to the Great Chief. The Chief, by special messenger, will pass it on to the girl's parents. If the proposal is accepted, the parents will collect the customary presents and place them on the threshold of the young man's hut. These presents constitute, so to speak, the dowry—household utensils, tools, blankets, oil lamps, pieces of material, mats;

everything in fact necessary for setting up house. A girl may also make her own choice, which she communicates to her parents, and if they approve, they also go and lay down the trousseau for the future bridegroom.

A marriage is always a very important occasion, celebrated with great festivities and ceremonies. In the eyes of the bride and bridegroom not only has a wedding a sacred character, but it is also an exchange of solemn oaths in the presence of a great number of people. And these people will be witnesses as to how those oaths are kept. The whole tribe, and sometimes members of neighbouring tribes, are invited. A husband's attitude toward his wife is a mixture of affection, respect and firmness. Quarrels are disapproved of, but it is admitted that they sometimes occur and are even sometimes quite acrimonious. In these cases Custom prescribes that the relations, friends and neighbours should do their best to effect a reconciliation between husband and wife. The two must pardon one another and offer a banquet to the peacemakers—in sign of gratitude and contrition.

There are no women members of the council of Elders, and women do not take part in the political discussions which sometimes precede the meeting of the Word, to which they are invited as of right. If they are not consulted they are regularly informed. They can individually apply to the Great Chief when they wish to submit a complaint to him, which, however, cannot be taken into consideration unless it is obviously of a serious character and husband, father or brother are not competent to deal with it. Divorce, practically speaking, does not exist, and only one case has been known at Mouli of a crime of jealousy.

It is a higher civilization than ours. What did Ignace say? 'Men are men . . .' That is the secret! It is true he added, 'Women are women', but let us forget about that.

'a white octopus killed by a bite from Alphonse'
overleaf: 'their way of life is an enactment of poetry'

24 *The Weather that is Master*

'JUST our luck!' I shouted in disgust as I ran into the fragile palm-leaf shelter where Benoît was working on the rib of a boat. I stood just under the roof and pointed to the sky, now again overcast.

'Do you think we'll be able to go out tomorrow?'

'The weather is master.'

I was once again struck by his quiet tone—so much in harmony with the calm strength he displayed in his work. It was a moment when, I think for the first time on Mouli, I felt myself rather a stranger . . . just a traveller, his stock of surprise soon exhausted, but now beginning to open his eyes on to himself.

For a week the westerly gale had blown ceaselessly and I had been waiting with increasing impatience for it to become fine. A heavy swell was still surging on to the beach. The boats, sprinkled with driven sand, were hauled up dry at the top of the strand, supported by their palm-trunk props. Every grey, rainy morning put off the expedition we had planned.

Pierre Dumai, Génio, Néophyte, Ignace, Guy, Victor, Alphonse, Benoît and I were to go off and explore a famous sandy shallows some distance away where there were giant clams. We were to go in two boats to fish at night on this stretch and we would get back to Mouli only at dawn on the second day.

I was looking forward to an exciting time. I could hardly contain my impatience. I had brought my travel-diary up to date (. . . 'a tropical paradise must have excess in all things. Here rain is tolerable only in short, severe storms, etc. . . .'). I wandered over the island, unable to settle down to anything.

'when I get back, I shall be homesick for Mouli'

A fine bright spell gave me renewed hope, but more wind and rain soon dashed it. It was then I felt I must seek comfort from one of my future fellow-adventurers.

'The weather is master.' He was of course just as anxious as I was for the sun and fine weather which would allow us to put to sea, but he accepted this truth as a fundamental fact, putting aside all impatience, all unnecessary bad humour and leaving him at liberty to dream, to contemplate—or to get on with the work in hand.

My restlessness was quite useless. What influence could it have except on me? I assumed that, if something had been decided on, then of course it must take place. Benoît had not destroyed my system, but he had, in one short phrase, proved to me to what extent it was only a system. Benoît *possessed* a philosophy, since he applied it. I only imagined that I possessed one.

Benoît put down his plane and looked up from the smooth, fresh piece of wood as he released the now finished rib from the vice.

'Maybe the day after tomorrow. There's a change of the moon.'

Travel Notes A coasting vessel from Nouméa had landed a few cases of food and also some things I had left in Colliard's boat—including my transistor. She took on board as much copra as was in sacks—and then left. This evening, while listening to some music, I was able to put into words something I felt as I watched that old tub vanish beyond the passage. The music was Bach. That orderly gush of sound, that divine mathematics, that progression to infinity—it was impossible not to associate the music's message with that rusty old hulk, which had nevertheless become a symbol of the outside world.

What I was suffering from was homesickness. 'You are only a traveller,' the young priest had said.

The weather that is master

With the new moon came a distinct change of weather. Many stars now, and the crashing of the surf has died away. Perhaps we shall start tomorrow.

25 *The Giant Clams*

IGNACE, at the helm of the first of the two boats, was plotting something. Ever since we had begun to skirt the steep shore of the deserted islet, he had been exchanging mysterious faces with the other men, knowing signals I could not help noticing despite my blissful torpor. I was lying on the bows stretched out in the sunshine. But still, what could those conspirators' looks mean?

'Look out! Look out!' warned Ignace. 'Over there, do you see it?'

I jumped up. What was the matter with him?

'Quick, look! Look carefully, very carefully! Salute to the General!'

The promontory of the islet we were now almost past looked like a gigantic ship's figure-head. From a certain angle, it represented with astonishing accuracy the face of General de Gaulle, with something of the proud bearing of one inspired by austere thoughts and given over to grandiose imaginings.

Gutzon Borglum carved on the sides of Mount Rushmore a hundred times larger than life-size, the faces of the most eminent men in American history—Washington, Jefferson, Lincoln and Theodore Roosevelt. I am in a position to inform General de Gaulle's biographers that nature has undertaken to do for him what Borglum did for the Americans. I am inclined to believe that some people, if they learn of this revelation will see in it a predestination. After all, although it is in the antipodes, the rock is nevertheless in French territory. One thing is sure, the people of Ouvéa have no need to erect a monument to the glory of their President—it already exists, and they would be hard put to it to create one more true to life—or more full of poetry.

We sailed along, under a warm, light wind, for about another hour, before a great green patch showed from far off the site of the sandy shallows that were the goal of our leisurely navigation.

It was from the Red Sea that the first of the giant bivalve molluscs were sent to the West, where they took their name of 'holy-water stoops' (in French *bénitiers*). The Arab, Sudanese or Erythrean fellahin who hauled up on to their sambuks the weighty shells that they had prized off the seabed, can hardly have imagined they were, if only indirectly, taking part in the worship of infidels.

Perhaps many of us have seen an under-water photograph taken by the Austrian Hans Hass in the depths of the Great Barrier Reef and showing a plaster leg (from a shop-window dummy) held tight between the two shells of a huge *tridacna*.[1] It is a photograph at once horrible and quaint—Salvador Dali and the dangers of the sea. As a matter of fact this particular danger is more potential than real. Since it is fixed to the seabed the *tridacna* can neither move nor seize the smallest object which does not place itself within its reach. The *tridacna* feeds on drifting plankton and the stories about it are just legends—it can never be an aggressor. When it is attacked it is protected by the impenetrable thickness of its two shells clamped together. The notched, serrated sides of the two halves form a terrible vice—an instrument of death indeed, but only in the case of an odd sort of suicide, or of carelessness so unlikely it would border on madness.

Once when I was in the neighbourhood of the New Hebrides and I was chatting about sea-shells with the second officer of

---

(1) The scientific name of the giant clam. The photograph not only appeared in a popular magazine but was also reproduced in Hass's book *We come from the Sea*.

a small vessel making its way painfully toward the island of Mallicolo, the young half-caste suddenly called out to one of the native divers, the oldest of the crew. I could not understand much of the dialogue, since it was in 'bêche-de-mer' patois, but it was lively. The diver shook his fuzzy head several times in absolute refusal, and he was imitated by all his companions. The second insisted, but quite in vain. He came back shrugging his shoulders.

'What's going on?'

'I asked these fools to take us to a bed where it seems there is a giant clam over six feet across. It has been there for ever practically. I would have liked to show it to you, since you are interested in such contraptions, but there's nothing doing. They are mortally afraid of it.'

'It's absurd. What are they frightened of? They'd have to shove themselves inside it.'

'I know, but in the islands there are lots of stories about giant clams and these fools take them for gospel truth. It'd be easier to get them dive in with a dozen tiger-sharks.'

'More than six feet across?' I was sceptical.

'Well, perhaps. It's never been measured. But go and take a look at the *baléze* they've got on show at Port-Vila in front of the Government building.'

The next day I was on land and went to look at the specimen that is famous throughout the archipelago. One of this *tridacna's* shells was eight inches thick and could easily have served me as a bath-tub.

Some of the many species of *tridacna* are no larger than a man's hand. These are most abundant on shallow coral beds, sometimes so abundant that they seem to cover the seabed. The flesh of this mollusc, with the sinuous lips of its shell, is particularly vividly coloured—as though pigmented with phosphorus.

Once, on the *Moana* expedition, we berthed alongside the burning, pebbly soil of Touamotou. The Manihi atoll offered an astounding spectacle. As we looked toward the interior of the lagoon the coral plateau that bordered on the passage spread into an immense scintillating expanse, pastel rose and blue. The delicate material of the coral was bathed in water so limpid that had it not been for the multicoloured parrot-fish darting about we would not have noticed it. The corals were everywhere encrusted with *tridacnas* opening their phosphorescent mouths to the golden sunlight of the transparent water—ruby, purple, scarlet, garnet-red, vermilion, madder, jade, turquoise, emerald, malachite, lapis-lazuli, aquamarine, chalcedony, azurite, amethyst . . . jewels of flesh in their mounts, a horizontal stained-glass window radiant, flashing, sparkling as far as the blue frontier of the depths.

Sometimes the giant clams are enveloped on the beds by spreading corals. Then you need a miner's bar to wrench them loose. Others lie on sand and only their weight prevents a diver from bringing up with him these massive objects, as much as forty-five, sixty or maybe even ninety pounds—sometimes indeed more than that.

The giant clam's flesh is a delicacy the men of Mouli procure in a very ingenious fashion:

Mathias has just finished coiling a rope. Benoît, at the bow, knotted it at the end round the point of a small stick. Then he put on his wooden goggles.

'You're ready?'

I fixed on my submarine mask.

We jumped overboard, Benoît taking the rope as it uncoiled. A *tridacna* opened. Twenty-five feet below the surface and on the sand, the clam seemed enormous. I noticed that Benoît dived so that he did not intercept the sun's rays striking the bottom. The giant mollusc was yawning up to them. The *tridacna* is a photoelectric cell: the slightest variation in the intensity of light on the membrane that joins the two halves of the shell causes them to snap together at once. The muscle that operates this movement is of fantastic strength. When

the retractile lips began to curl, Benoît pushed in the rope
with the help of the little stick and then snatched the stick out
before it was crushed. He gave one or two sharp jerks upwards
on the rope and then a long pull downwards—a signal to
Mathias—and we surfaced. At the same time the prize was
hauled aboard. So simple.

'You have only got to think of it! Very clever.'

Benoît smiled. It was surprising what little things amazed
me.

'Now you try.'

But it was not quite so easy as it looked. In my haste, I let
the little stick graze the edge of a shell and in a fraction of a
second the mollusc snapped shut. I stayed down on the bottom
and waited for it to come ajar again, but all I managed was to
nearly suffocate.

'Too quick,' said Benoît as we surfaced. 'Have another try.'

Another miss. The clam snapped shut before I got near it
even. I asked my teacher for another demonstration. With a
deftness and a precision the water made all the more remarkable, Benoît slipped in his cord, and another prize was heaved
up to the daylight. I made a third attempt, and I was so sure
I would fail that just the contrary happened.

Much later on I was to write in my note-book:

'Marvellous how easily these creatures (some of whose
shells were twenty inches across) were gathered—I cannot
think of any other term except "picked", and that is just as
wrong. Then I got to thinking about how decorative these
shells would be in a house. A diving campaign. A thousand
tridacnas. But how could one transport thirty or forty tons?
And how could one keep intact such relatively fragile objects?
The inside of the shells looks as though it were made of the
finest marble and it shares a marble's hardness, but the edges
are brittle. Benoît, pushing the blade of his matchet between
the edges, before I could stop him, to cut the muscle of an

enormous clam that was half opening on board, damaged the
brittle part that forms the undulating fringe of the jaws.
Anyway I am still thinking about it. It would be a good
opportunity (and a pretext) for going back to Europe. Commerce? Yes, of course. But it would combine passion for the
sea with a business I could handle. At Mouli I am just a
parasite, a sort of Ginger Ted[1] who drinks only coconut milk
and tea. No use trying to fool myself about that, even if the
council of Elders and Pierre Dumai swear it is not true.'

---

(1) An incorrigible 'soak', beach-combing on a Pacific island
before being 'saved' by the sister of the missionary, his deadly
enemy.

26 Sharks and Paradise

With his feet in the water and his arms outstretched, Victor stood motionless, closely following the movements of a young shark that had been attracted by the bits of food we had thrown into the small, sandy creek after our meal. But the little creature was suspicious and kept his distance.

'You'll miss him,' said Ignace ironically—like the rest of us, he was lying down not far from the water's edge—'You'd miss it if it was a sperm-whale.'

No answer from Victor. His back was turned and his harpoon poised.

'Be careful,' went on Ignace. 'Be careful. The other leg . . .'

'Fool.'

'Fool yourself,' went on Ignace . . . and what anyone was going to say next was drowned in the general hubbub. Victor had hurled his harpoon. The barb had stuck in a branchial slit. The shark vanished in a thick cloud of blood with the shaft of the harpoon jerking about above. Victor grabbed hold of another and flung it. But he kept at a prudent distance. Victor's carefulness was quite justified: often a young shark's reaction is to counterattack, whereas a fully-grown one will make off. In fact, Victor had had a bitter experience a few years earlier.

He was fishing for mullet along the shore when a shark, not more than three feet long, glided up to snatch a fish impaled on the point of Victor's spear. Victor was in the water up to his waist and, without shifting his position, threw his spear. It grazed a fin and then stuck in the sand. The young shark, infuriated, swished around, charged and snapped at Victor's thigh. He balled his fist and hammered on the shark's flat head. After a few moments the creature let go and streaked away. A slice of Victor's flesh was just hanging by the skin. He cut it off and went and buried it in the cemetery under a heap of sand with a small cross on it. Then he hid for two weeks, waiting for the herbal dressing to heal the wound.

'You've still got the mark?' I asked.

He pulled up his *parāu* and showed me a dreadful scar. An inch or two higher and it would have severed the femoral artery.

'It was all your own fault,' said Benoît in his usual slow, level-headed manner. 'There's no need to stick your spear into a shark—especially a little one—but if you do you've got to be sure not to miss. Sharks don't often bite men,' he added. 'Sometimes when we're fishing from the shore and there are sharks about they'll come up quite near our legs, but they never bite us, even the biggest ones. Sharks are like us,' he concluded. 'They eat fish. Leave a shark alone and he doesn't bother you.'

'That's true,' Néophyte added. 'Even today at Saint-Joseph[1] sharks are taboo for the older men.'

'And not only at Saint-Joseph,' put in Pierre Dumai. 'At Mouli too.' He turned to me. 'There is still a shark that helps the Saint-Joseph and Mouli men in the boat on the open sea, and he's being doing that ever since the Ancestors came here in canoes.'

I did not say anything for a minute.

'Is that a legend?'

'No, it really happened, and it still does.'

I opened a packet of cigarettes and offered them round. Though I do not usually smoke, this time I lit one.

'Out with it.'

'If you like.'

Pierre inhaled several times and then put down his cigarette.

'When the father and son called Mamu and Nemunu came from Wallis with the other canoes, they had on board a god

---

(1) Saint-Joseph is an island opposite Mouli in the Ouvéa atoll.

147

in a basket, and all the time they were guided by a fire on the sea. First of all there they were off *Grande Terre* on the Wailou side. Their sail was torn and they mended it on a sandy islet. When night fell, the fire moved about on the sea, so they got into the canoes again and at last they reached Ouvéa. There Mamu felt he was going to die, and they laid him down on the beach. Then he said, "In a short while I shall be dead. You will cut off my head and go and bury it on the sandy islet where we first touched. But before you do that you must throw my body into the passage, otherwise you will not see any fire." Then Mamu died and Nemunu obeyed his father's last wishes. He had Mamu's head cut off and put into a basket on the largest canoe. Nemunu threw the body into the passage. Immediately a large shark appeared alongside the canoe and guided the men, and they soon saw a fire. Sometimes they did not see it any more, then the shark came to guide them again. After a few times they declared that the shark was taboo. Since that time the men of Saint-Joseph and Mouli who are descended from Mamu and Nemunu see a big shark when they cross over in the direction of Wailou, and then very soon they see a fire.'

'A fire on land?'

'A fire on land, that can be seen far out at sea.'

'Isn't it a lighthouse?'

'There's a government fire, but it's the same thing.'

We looked up at the carangues hunting right on the shore. The tight-packed shoal of little, fleeing fish cut through the water with as much noise and as swiftly as the bow of a motor-boat.

'There are taboo sharks also at Tsiaboumbon,' said Génio with a smile.

'No, that's just a legend,' answered Pierre.

'Yes, it is a legend,' Génio admitted.

In dumb-show Ignace pointed up at the sky between the palm-trees.

'It's up there: Paradise.'

They all nodded their heads in agreement. I was puzzled.

'Génio, now it's your turn to tell us a story.'

'Suppose you're dead, but that you're living all the same—your soul. Then you swim as far as the coast of *Grande Terre*. There you see the taboo sharks, before you get to the way that leads to Tsiaboumbon. And the sharks go along with you. Before you arrive, look, there's one of the sharks that turns into an evil spirit, Kiéouma. This Kiéouma gets up on to a rock just before you reach Tsiaboumbon and throws out a net to catch souls. There's no way of escape. And the souls must suffer severely before Kiéouma calms down and lets them go. There's also a big madrepore you have to go under, but I've forgotten its name . . .'

'Diaraboua,' murmured Mathias.

'That's it, Diaraboua. You pass and there you are, your soul's at Tsiaboumbon. It's a country you cannot guess the size of. You can't express in words how big it is. It is more beautiful than mortal man can imagine, for its beauty is made only for souls. All the fruits, all the vegetables we know of and many others foreign to us, ripen as standing crops, in huge forests, and do not have to be tended. It isn't even necessary to pick them; you always find baskets full by the wayside, within hand's reach. The Great Chief is so tall that on earth he would reach up to the sky. His feet are petrified since he never moves. But this Chief, who is called Dobat or Doibat . . .'

'Doibat,' said Mathias.

'This Doibat sees everything that happens at Tsiaboumbon, and commands that all the souls shall be completely happy. For them no old age, no death, no sickness, no sorrow, nothing like that—eternal happiness for souls more numerous than the stars of heaven, who never tire of gazing at one another with admiration and love. So when someone on earth dies, there is great rejoicing, and their relations carry baskets of presents to await the arrival of the new soul.'

Génio, lost in the tale he was telling, smiled to himself.

'Paradise, that's what it is!—But it's under the sea, the Elders used to tell before the missionaries came.'

We turned on our elbows towards the crackling noise that came over the motionless water. The shoal of little fish was still fleeing before the carangues.

The sea under the setting sun was a sheet of oil ready to burst into flame. I closed my dazzled eyes. I was lying high up on a slope of shells and corals whitened and worn by the tides that washed the creek. The outlines of the two boats on which we were to sail still remained imprinted on my retina in a blaze of dancing dots; the silhouettes seemed black among a maze of moving, luminous objects.

'No wind,' said Alphonse. 'We'll have to row for a couple of hours.'

I opened my eyes and shaded them with my hands.

The men moving toward the boats were vague, blurred shadows . . .

27 Night Fishing

MATHIAS had stopped rowing. Small, phosphorescent bubbles were dribbling down the oars he had pulled from the rowlocks and put noiselessly under the gunwales. Not a breath of wind in the stormy air. The lambent flame of a great flash of lightning lit the face of a near-by islet. Then all was pitch-black again, save for the lantern of the second boat behind us and the feeble glimmer of our own storm-lantern casting a flicker on the lifeless water. Génio in the bow was dropping the anchor. The slight rattle as the links of the chain ran out intensified the silence.

'Twelve fathoms,' said Génio, turning to Benoît.

'All right. Let go.'

We were in fact over the bed in a place where, with a favourable moon, boats had taken a full cargo of fish in the space of three hours. But some had gone back home without any catch at all. A shoal of snappers was there or it was not.

Several flashes of lightning, one after the other. It was summer lightning—long-lasting, flickering streaks in the hot, tense atmosphere of the night.

Benoît cut a mackerel into strips on the gunwale. Néophyte got out the nylon lines, muttering stifled curses as he found them tangled. Then he handed them out to each one of us, baited his own and cast. The line went taut and he struck. His thick lips pressed together. His tense, bent body, his rippling muscles showed he was battling with a giant. I cast at the same time as Benoît. Néophyte pulled in nothing but a silver snapper no longer than his forearm. I felt a pull on my line and struck. It was a shark! Impossible to hold. The nylon line cut into my hand. Benoît had also struck.

'The shoal's there.' Benoît's voice was almost un-recognizable. 'Don't leave any slack.'

'It's a shark. I can't hold him.'

'Shark, my foot. It's a flat-nose. Don't leave any slack. Pull in at once!'

With both hands he hauled in a snapper that lashed about like the devil. On the gunwale it slipped its hook, leapt up from the deck, overthrew the brazier and the tea-pot and knocked against everything near it. Its strength was incredible and it made a noise like a machine-gun. Mathias smashed down on it with his matchet.

My line was so taut that it looked like breaking. No fish that weighed only about fifteen pounds could put up such a fight. Benoît hauled in another snapper. Then Ignace, Génio, Néophyte and Mathias all caught similar prizes, and they raised hell in the boat before they were clubbed to death. I felt the creature at the end of my line swerve in an arc and almost imperceptibly stop. Had it slipped the hook? Was the line broken? Then the pull became stronger than ever. My hand hurt so much that I was furious, and no doubt therefore gathered the necessary strength. I got the better of it. It was only a snapper. Benoît grabbed it by the gills before it reached the gunwale.

Other fish leapt up and flopped back on the deck with such cracks that they should have been stunned, if not brained. But it needed a good many blows with a matchet to kill them. They leapt about here, there and everywhere, thrashing and smashing with crazy energy.

I baited my line and cast. It shot through my hands with terrific speed. This could not possibly be a snapper. Benoît touched me on the shoulder.

'Go on. Pull in. Don't leave so much slack.'

'I can't, this time it really is a shark.'

'Not on your life, it's another flat-nose. Go on, haul in. I'll help. Look!'

With his fists close together, smoothly and with all his strength, he kept pulling, increasing the force by throwing all the weight of his body backwards. I felt my forearms trembling as I did the same, until we saw a glittering body emerge. A snapper. Benoît had been right.

'He pulls more than a six-foot shark.'

We baited and cast. The lines were always taken before they reached the bottom. There was no need for any special care. Hundreds of snappers, perhaps thousands, were under our keels, and they rushed at anything within their reach, fighting each other for a prize. The struggles could be felt at the end of the quivering lines. The fish were voracious, famished, battling for bits of food. Cast, strike, pull in.

Fitful lightning played overhead and the boat was bedlam. The slapping of the fish resounded on the decks. The catch piled up in the bows. Scales flew everywhere, into our eyes and mouths. I no longer noticed the pain in my hands. I seemed to be drawing on a form of life endowed with such strength and voracity as are unknown now in the animal world, creatures of a bygone age. They rushed on to the bait, dragged at it savagely with their abnormally powerful muscles. The hysteria of bodies too powerful for their size.

Suddenly there was a double tug, my pull and another against me at the end of the line.

'Shark,' said Benoît.

The resistance ceased. I hauled in the head of a snapper sheared off at the gills as if by a razor. Mathias's line was carried off and broke.

'Fishing's over.'

I pulled the head off my hook and threw it away. From far underneath a great phosphorescent mass arose. The tail of a comet. I turned to Benoît. 'Have you got the thick shark-line aboard?'

He shook his head.

'It's here all right, but it's no use. These are big ones.'

He hooked a snapper and let down his line, no more than a fathom. Once again the huge, luminous shape appeared. Benoît hauled in his bait slowly. The two gleaming points of green that followed it became the upright pupils of the eyes of a great tiger-shark as it rose from the water. It stared up at the snapper dangling above its wide head. Leviathan lured. By the feeble light of the lantern I could make out clearly the dark stripes on its slowly wriggling body as it made off. The gigantic tail smacked against the boat and splashed water over us.

Maybe before dawn the wind would rise. I was exhausted and half-starved. My hands were swollen and very painful, but I helped Néophyte as best I could to put things in order on board.

Mathias threw coconut fibre on the brazier, poured a little kerosene over it and set light to it. He cut two large fillets from a snapper, washed them against the side of the boat, drained the water off carefully before he laid them on a wire gridiron. The embers began to glow. We could see a few stars.

28 Sea Eagles

'FROM the top of the cliff?'

'Well, yes, right on top.'

For the second time the seagull dived on to the seething mass of mackerel in the net we were hauling up on the beach.

'It's not possible!'

Ignace, irritated by my incredulity, tossed his head impatiently.

'For the young people, yes, it's finished. They don't jump any more. But we older men, mark my words, we all do. All of us.'

I went on hauling but I stared at him with astonishment. Mathias behind him nodded his head in agreement.

'Watch out,' shouted Benoît from the other side of the net (the fish were jumping about). 'Pull quickly! Pull!'

Children on the beach were holding the ropes and pulling. Soon the net was on dry land. There were at least two hundred mackerel in it. We began to string them through the gills with pandanus lianas.

'I never heard you mention what you just told me,' I said to Ignace.

'Well, we're talking about it now. It was you who looked at the bird.'

'We don't jump often,' put in Benoît. 'Before, yes, often; now we are beginning to forget a bit. But we do still go now and then.'

'You'll be going? You'd take me with you?'

Benoît looked enquiringly at Ignace and Mathias.

'Maybe we'll go to the little island,' he agreed. 'We'll ask Néophyte and Alphonse to come with us.'

'When? Tomorrow?'

He thought over the times of the tides.

'Maybe tomorrow, or the day after. I'm going to sew the sail of my boat.'

'I'll help you with that if you like. That's something I do know how to do,' I added quickly.

If that seagull had not swooped down on a mackerel, and if I had not remarked on the bird's astonishing skill as it carried it off, I should not have prompted Ignace to say what he did, poking fun at my admiration of the seagull, and I should never have spent the unforgettable day which resulted from this.

Benoît put down a couple of nuts and looked over to where I was sewing the sail spread over my knees.

'Are you thirsty?'

'Well, I'd like a drink.'

He chopped the top off a nut and cut a square out of the tender white flesh. I took a long draught of the deliciously cool milk.

'You've seen Alphonse and Néophyte?'

'It's all right. They'll come.'

'When do we start?'

'Early tomorrow morning.'

'Tell me something about this fishing, if you've got time.'

He settled himself against a near-by coco-palm and pushed back the brim of his Anzac hat a little.

'When the tide covers the narrow coral reef at the foot of the cliffs, the sea-eagles begin to glide about looking for fish coming to the surface. Up till then, they've stayed in their eyries. Sometimes you see them fold their wings and swoop on their prey. They snatch the fish and carry it off in their claws.

'The Ancients spent a lot of time watching the sea-eagles fishing. The birds drop straight down, and they reckoned if they did that it was proof that nature had made fish vulnerable to this form of attack. And if sea-eagles had not been able to employ it, they would not exist, since they feed exclusively on fish. Generally speaking, the eagles dropped down from a great height, but quite often the drop was a matter of only thirty feet or so. A man can fall into the sea from such a height, so why could not a man do what a bird did? Some men can see in the dark; others can make out a canoe three or four hours' sail away from the village; and others can plug a spear ten times running into a coconut a good distance off. Of course, men have not got claws, but harpoons hardened in the fire will pierce the flesh of the largest fish easier than the long, curved claws of birds.

'So there developed the idea of this sort of fishing where men armed with long poles with hardened trident heads fixed to them jumped from the top of the cliffs on to the fish. From that time, you may say, men themselves became Sea Eagles—surpassing the great birds of prey in strength and courage, since men went so far as to attack sharks, and that no bird can do.

'Men are always strongest,' went on Benoît. 'Even the biggest shark in creation, well, you make a large hook and tie it on to a thick rope—and there you are! Even whales. It's true we Mouli men never went after whales, but at Lifou and Maré in the old days . . . the old men on the whalers . . ' (he imitated the throwing of a heavy harpoon) 'a good shot right on the head and there you are.'

Dark night waters absolutely still under fading stars. We had to row a little toward the interior of the lagoon and then our sail caught the slight breeze that rose with a radiant sun. A few minutes later we were sailing free in ideal conditions—a brisk but not too strong wind blowing in the right direction over a sea as yet untroubled by swell.

I noticed Benoît staring up at the square of coarse canvas

I knew I had sewn securely right in the middle of the bellying sail. He saw I was watching him and he grinned with satisfaction.

'Damn patch . . .'

'Well, it'll never tear'—a compliment from Ignace.

'Would take a cyclone.' Néophyte went one better.

'You old fool,' said Ignace. 'If there was a cyclone the sail would be furled hours before . . .'

'How do you know? You've never seen a cyclone. And if you did you'd go and hide in a cave with the crabs.'

We all laughed aloud. For once Néophyte had got even with Ignace.

The creek on the leeward of the island where we left the cutter formed a sort of tiny, natural port. Zanclus and other butterfly-fish darted about in the transparent blue water. We scrambled over a slope of rocks to the top. As I paused to take breath, I watched the ballet of small coloured fish. Beyond the lagoon, the boundless stretch of the beach merged into the horizon.

Benoît led the way along the top of the cliffs. You could not cut across the islet because it was covered with impenetrable scrub. We had to go round the edge to reach the windy side where there were most fish. My companions marched with bare feet on the jagged stone with astonishing agility. They moved without difficulty or hesitation, with their long spears over their shoulders—and amused themselves by scaring the lizards or by disturbing the many black-ringed yellow or blue snakes with their toes.

Not one of these Sea Eagles was less than fifty-four. That was Benoît's age, and he was the youngest. Alphonse was fifty-six, Ignace and Néophyte both sixty-one, and I knew that Mathias was certainly sixty-six—a slender white-haired athlete, who had practised this sort of fishing for forty-eight years.

Layers of palm-leaves and nuts from the wild cocos had

covered the limestone with a strong-smelling humus. But the smell left us when we faced into the wind and we soon got to a wide open position on the cliff. There were traces of fire in front of a small palm-leaf hut. The men stacked their weapons and then looked over the cliff to judge the state of the tide. I felt slightly giddy as I too leaned over from a smooth, sheer spur of rock. Right down below the branching corals were only just covered by a gently lapping tide. Another eight inches and it would reach the top of the rocks' discoloration, the line marking high-water level.

The men were going to jump from a very considerable height. Was not this sort of fishing dangerous? Were not they afraid of accidents? Benoît admitted that one man had been killed, though it was really his own fault. Nothing would have happened if he had jumped the right way. He had played the fool and kicked his legs about as he jumped, so that he could not avoid getting splayed out. His spear hit the water at the wrong angle and broke in two, and a prong of his trident went into his head.

Benoît took a firm grip of his harpoon and showed me exactly how it had to be used. The right hand must clasp the shaft high up and at the same time press it firmly against the left thigh, and the left hand help keep it there. The trident must strike the fish downwards and at a slight angle. The weapon was never thrown, but kept very tightly pressed against the body. The falling man is just a deadweight.

Just before they took up their positions on the edge of the cliff, I asked them to warn me before they jumped so that I would not miss any phases of the operation. From their silence I hadn't gathered that my request was unreasonable. Events were to show me that it was.

The five men were equally spaced on a front of about fifty yards. I kept close to Mathias in the middle. Suddenly Néophyte on the left shouted:

'The big parrot! There! There! Look out!'

Then he was in the air. He made a great noise as he struck the water, and this brought a slight expression of disapproval to Mathias's face. A trained and experienced Sea Eagle should hit the water with less noise. All the same, Néophyte reappeared triumphant, with a magnificent parrot-fish skewered on his trident.

I was astounded. But the feat of spearing the fish was almost equalled by that of Néophyte's climb up the steep side of the cliff. He had not only muscles of steel, but the most exceptional strength in his hands, and an ability to fit his body round the slightest protuberance, however little marked, and to make use of it. He pulled in his belly and supported himself on his chest, and then clutched a thin edge with the finger-tips of his right hand—his left held his trident and fish. Then, from that position, he crawled up perpendicularly about eighteen inches to a less unfavourable place. I don't know how he did it. In fact what I was watching was a skill equal to that of the legendary 'lizard-men', whose exploits I had heard tell about in the Leeward Islands.[1] The bodies of certain chiefs, and even their canoes, were deposited in bygone times in open grottoes on the giddy, tall cliffs of Moorea and Maupiti. Now I understood how.

Néophyte reached the top. He straightened up without asking for help. There was no puffing or blowing. He showed me the fine blue-green fish, as long as his arm. The fins and tail, like a 'U' upside down, were brilliant with all shades of orange and purple.

'No time to wait,' he smiled, as though in excuse. 'When the fish is there, there it is, and you jump.'

'*Bécune*'[2] murmured Mathias a few paces off. He was motionless. I went over to him.

---

(1) Not the Leeward Islands in the West Indies, but what the French call *Les Iles sous le Vent*, a group to the north of Tahiti.
(2) That is, 'barracuda'.

Try as I would, I could not make out a thing. But Mathias fixed his eyes on one place where the surface was rippling. Before I saw the long fish catch the light, Mathias was in the air. The impact seemed to cut the fish in two. It and the man disappeared in a spurt of spray. Great rings of foam grew wider and wider before Mathias' white hair reappeared, and then the barracuda dead on the trident. Mathias swam away a little and landed on the coral reef. His catch was too heavy for him to haul up with him. Benoît threw down a long, flexible liana which Mathias slipped through the barracuda's gills and carefully knotted. I helped Benoît to pull it up. It was bathed in blood. The three prongs had entered the back so violently that their joints (where they were strengthened by coiling copper wire round the shaft) had ploughed a deep, circular wound in the broken backbone. A hundred and fifty pounds behind the trident. A human bomb. Struck in this way any animal would be killed on the spot.

It was not that I had doubted what Benoît had told me the day before, but now I understood that in this way a man *could* kill a shark.

'You could catch one like that?' I asked Ignace as he was staring at a shoal of surgeon-fish swimming in close to the shore.

'Smaller than that.'

There is always something in Ignace's attitude that encourages one to challenge him.

'I'd like to see that very much indeed.'

He glanced at me, half-ironically, half-offended.

'Wait a minute. Come with me.'

He walked a few paces along the top of the cliff.

'Do you see that one?'

'The yellow one with red stripes next to the blue coral?'

'That's the fellow.'

What Ignace was claiming to be able to do was about the

same as hurling a javelin from a considerable distance on to a playing-card. However, there he was getting ready to jump, screwing up his eyes in concentration, biting his lip and watching every movement of the little fish nearly forty feet below him. Then he leapt. For a moment I thought he had missed. But no, he really had speared the one he aimed at, no bigger than a man's hand—the only zanclus in a shoal of butterfly-fish. From up above I made obvious signs of contrition which seemed to satisfy him, for he left off brandishing his weapon and began to swim to the sea's edge.

The others were far off following the movements of some carangues after a shoal of little fish. I had stayed near Mathias. He looked like a peaceful shepherd leaning on his crook, lost in contemplation of the sea. He seemed carelessly at ease, but he was prepared for action. Slowly he raised his left arm.

'What's the matter, Mathias?'

Without saying anything or even looking at me, he pointed with his chin to something I managed to make out in the thick coral bushes, made iridescent by the little waves. A huge moray eel emerged from a crack. It was clear from the way it moved forward so swiftly that it was preparing to leave its lair. Did Mathias really intend to attack it? How would he manage? It seemed impossible to me. Moray eels never venture out into open water. They will follow an ebb tide when they want to change their lairs; or they will swim close to corals and then go back into their holes.

If this creature moved toward our right it would gain the shelter of the broad projections of rock that extended like eaves over the sea. If it went to the left it would have to wriggle its way for a very short distance in the open sea from a breach in the barrier reef . . . above which Mathias had gone to take up his position. The long, dark, yellow-blotched ribbon undulated along, perpendicular to the wall. The black head hesitated for a moment, and then the moray swerved to the left.

I could not say that Mathias had jumped or that he had taken aim at any particular moment, or judged the angle of his fall. He just let himself drop, almost exactly in the position in which he stood. All I noticed was a slight push of his left heel against the rock. He brushed the corals and plunged into the water. He remained under the surface for what seemed endless seconds. I could not help feeling agonizingly anxious. Maybe he was wounded. Maybe he was struggling with the gigantic eel. Perhaps a secret pride had driven him to attempt an impossible feat to impress someone he knew admired the skill of the Sea Eagles. Had he not taken undue risks? . . No, he had just been swimming under the water and was now getting a foothold on a clump of madrepore coral. The moray eel, to all appearances dead, floated from the end of the harpoon Mathias was quietly pulling along behind him.

It had been struck where its body was widest—that part of the neck just below the mouth where it swells like a monstrous goitre. The strength of the morays defies belief. This specimen, about four and a half feet long and certainly as thick through as Mathias's thigh, did not die at once. From so violent, and so accurate a blow, it was only stunned. Despite its gaping wounds, it tried to wriggle off the prongs, to bite them, to coil itself furiously around the harpoon, struggling and thrashing about in all directions. I threw a liana down to Mathias. He widened one of the wounds with his forefinger and tied the liana at the side of the creature's mouth. With great difficulty I hauled the long, limp body up the cliff, and Mathias clambered up without for a moment losing his calm, almost lazy ease of manner. The moray eel was now, admittedly, like all the other victims of the Sea Eagles—it was undoubtedly dead.

Benoît and Néophyte came back, carrying between them a leopard-ray so heavy it bowed the harpoon hafts they bore on their shoulders. Ignace and Alphonse had speared a carangue each.

The octopus, moving in open water, reached the wall and took up its position at a depth of hardly three feet. It spread out both mantle and tentacles over the coral and instantly assumed the same salmon-pink colour.

Ignace and I were standing together. We leant forward, and he pursed his lips and shook his head from side to side.

'Never in your life. The octopus can't win. The beak of the eagle will cut off his head below the eyes. Finished. Dead octopus.'

'The octopus will hide its head. And it's also got a beak—a beak that could bite the eagle,' put in Alphonse.

We were all gathered above the spot where the octopus was ensconced.

'Never on your life. The eagle can't win. The octopus will squirt ink and the eagle won't be able to see anything. Then it'll twist up two or three arms to protect its head, and then three or four arms to grab the eagle's wings . . . that's the end. The eagle will be pulled into the sea and drowned.'

It was I who had suggested a fight between the two creatures. Their joining battle would have a sort of symbolic significance. A mythological duel. The marine Hydra and the Bird-God. Although such a fight seemed to me to be incredibly bizarre and improbable, none of the human Sea Eagles had any doubt about its possibility. What they did not agree on was who would be the winner.

'And what's your opinion?' I asked Mathias. 'Which would win?'

Mathias did not answer. He just pointed to the octopus. It was beginning to make a move: it raised its mantle and at the same time changed its colour; it folded in its arms, blew up its pouch and slithered off the coral.

Despite the distance the octopus had already covered in

one movement, Alphonse jumped. In his haste his blow was
not very well aimed. Only one prong pierced the creature.
Then both it and Alphonse vanished in the cloud of sepia.
Gradually the water cleared and we saw that Alphonse's
shoulders were wrapped round with tentacles. He was not
even trying to pull them off. What was he waiting for? Was
he paralysed by other tentacles we could not see? Then, quite
calmly, as though taking a bite from an apple, he opened his
mouth and bit the octopus on the head. Its tentacles waved
and twisted convulsively, and it ejected another cloud of
sepia, but Alphonse did not let go until its arms fell lifeless.
A white octopus killed by a bite from Alphonse.

A few kitchen utensils were kept lying about on the floor
of the hut. Among them was an old rusted matchet that
Néophyte cleaned by pushing it several times into the earth.
The men were lying at their ease, but it was obvious they
were disappointed. It was not that they attached any great
importance to catching some special prize. There was always
the element of luck. But the tide had turned without our
getting a single shark and my companions seemed to be
regretting they had not been able to show me just how daring
they could be.

I could say nothing that would not ring false. Néophyte
cut and trimmed some branches, gathered a good many dry
coconuts, split them in two and put them on the ashes of the
old fire. Like tinder the fibrous husks spurted into flame.
Néophyte drove his stakes into the ground, placed two long,
straight sticks in their forks and laid across several twigs of
equal length to support the fish over the fire. The perfumed
smell of green wood mingled with the odour from the cooking
of the wounded fish. I stayed my hunger a little by chewing
small bits of copra pulled from a nut lying nearby. There was
complete silence. Ignace shot out a spurt of spittle that sizzled
on the embers.

'It's always like that. You don't want sharks and the sea is full of 'em. You do want a shark and you can be sure you never see a damned one.'

'Maybe the moon?' suggested Benoît.

He lit a cigarette from the fire, inhaled deeply and stretched out once more, his hands crossed on a stone behind his head.

'We'll try again at the next tide,' he went on. 'Maybe that'll be better.'

No one said anything. I had not dared to hope they would agree to stop on the islet and start all over again. We would be taking a risk if we spent the night at sea and got back to the cutter only at twilight, when the wind had dropped. As far as I personally was concerned, I would have gladly rowed all the way back to Mouli rather than miss seeing once again the fantastic spectacle of which I was the sole, privileged spectator.

'Shark,' said Mathias in a low voice.

A shark was swimming parallel to the cliff, its long, undulating shape not far below the surface. The men were all ready to jump, but it was out of reach. I could not see clearly enough to make out the species, but it was more than six feet long. I felt rather relieved when the great shadow moved away and disappeared. When it had come to seeing the actual event, my enthusiasm had faded. But my companions, far from being afraid of it, were now disappointed it had disappeared. Though I had been frightened for their sakes, I was also a little ashamed of myself. What I was so anxious to see was in fact worthy of the Roman circus. And I should be sitting safely in my vantage point while a gladiator would be perhaps risking his life.

Mathias had walked away. Now here he was with a huge hunk of ray which he began to fasten to a liana.

'That'll bring him back,' Benoît declared.

Ray's flesh smells strongly of ammonia: it's the best bait for sharks.

'I think we'd better go home and leave the sharks alone.'

The men looked at me in astonishment. Did I think they were acting just from bravado?

'We'll try,' said Benoît. 'If he doesn't come, then we'll go.'

Mathias lowered the piece of ray into the water. I no longer now felt as I had done only a few minutes before. It was clear now that my companions were themselves filled with excitement.

We did not have to wait long. The shark appeared again and drove straight at the bait. He sniffed at it and swerved away. His dorsal fin and the end of his tail were out of the water, sweeping round in a wide circle. Seen as it was from above no shark's outline had ever seemed to me so perfect. That compact, beautifully stream-lined body gave an impressive and dangerous sensation of power. The creature was suspicious. We could tell from its movements the struggle it was waging with its own greed. You might have thought: It was like a high precision engine irresistibly drawn to a magnet. Mathias murmured something. The shark came straight towards us, resolutely attacking. We could see his mouth above the surface, wide open to grab the bait.

Benoît jumped. His fall seemed endless; and the dull sound of shattered backbone reached us before the splash of man and shark going under. For a long time a cupola of bubbles hid them in the middle of the eddies.

The water still seethed when we saw the lifeless shark, and Benoît close against it. A double liana was thrown out to him. He gained a foothold and tied them together at the root of the shark's tail. We pulled on the carcass, taking care it should not knock against the cliff. A bump could easily snap the lianas, already stretched almost to breaking-point. It was a female blue shark (*Carcharinus*). Benoît's blow had struck the middle of the spine and killed it at once. Two baby sharks came prematurely from the opened belly, their mouths already furnished with plenty of needle-sharp teeth. They were so lively that Benoît, when he examined his booty, had great difficulty in cutting through the umbilical placenta. He threw the little sharks into the water and they set off swimming side by side.

A huge sun still hung above the line of the horizon. On our way back to the cutter, we were illuminated for a few moments by its last rays and we glistened red as fire while we marched along the edge of the cliff.

29 *On the Beach*

AN extraordinary sunset had just faded, the most beautiful
I had ever seen in the tropics. But it had appeared to me as
almost commonplace: while I watched it, I was thinking how
I should describe it later. My mind, preoccupied with what I
was going to do in the future, refused simply to enjoy the
scene. Emotion became tarnished as soon as I determined to
translate it into words—in fact, to utilize it. And how can
one translate emotion without being unfaithful to its essence
and reality?

What was the good of wanting to write a book? Would it
not be enough to experience the adventure of my stay here,
to live it out?

I was beginning to understand the purely instinctive
reasons that had induced me to write in an earlier book that
art is the active form of prayer.

30 Departure

The chiefs were so much attached to our people, that they rather encouraged their stay among them than otherwise, and even made them promises of large possessions. Under these and many other attendant circumstances, equally desirable, it is now perhaps not so much to be wondered at, though scarcely possible to have been foreseen, that a set of sailors, most of them void of connections, should be led away; especially when, in addition to such powerful inducements, they imagined it in their power to fix themselves in the midst of plenty, on one of the finest islands in the world, where they need not labour, and where the allurements of dissipation are beyond anything that can be conceived.

Captain Bligh, of *The Bounty*.

SOONER or later the problem had to be faced and I was grateful to Pierre Dumai for mentioning it.

'You're going to stay on Mouli?'

'I think now perhaps I ought to go back to my own country.'

He sipped at his tea.

'If you like we'll build you a big cabin. You can choose where you'd like it. I've spoken about it to the Elders and everyone has agreed.'

I knew what my answer would have to be.

'I'm very proud that you've made me that offer, but I can't accept, Pierre. I'm only a traveller.'

'Yes, I understand. You want to leave soon?'

'Next week.'

'A boat will take you to Fayawe, you've only to say what day.'

We were silent for a little while.

'I'm homesick for my country, Pierre, but I feel that when I get back there I shall be homesick for Mouli. Only for

Mouli. Nowhere else. Maybe I'll come back here.'

'Then you will be welcome again.'

The first Europeans who came to Mouli, in June 1848, were missionaries in *Arche de l'Alliance* commanded by Captain Marceau. They owed their lives, simply and solely, to the knowledge, the very imperfect knowledge, of the local dialect that was possessed by a Wallisian sailor. He had understood what the apparently peaceable and well-disposed native chief had said. It was 'Let them all land, then we'll kill them, eat them and seize their belongings.'

Arche de l'Alliance put out to sea again and the conversion of the islanders was delayed.

It was this interrupted landing and the banquet that never was that the *pilou* dancers were miming at the end of a feast in the court of the Big House. There was a roar of laughter from the long row of trestle tables when Ignace, painted in fearsome fashion and brandishing the last polished stone axe the tribe possessed, jumped on to me and pretended to smash in my skull, smacking his lips in a very significant way.

But this was the only cheerful note. From the morning of this last day sadness had been on every face. Pierre Dumai, Génio, Benoît, Alphonse, Ignace—with tears in his eyes—Victor, Néophyte, Guy . . . All the other men and the women on the edge of the beach. . . . I shook hands and we all realized that a bond had been created between them and me. My boat was bobbing on the waves and I was about to leave. These men and women were my friends, and I was their friend. I hope that this friendship will remain unbroken after they read this book. Their way of life is an enactment of poetry.

As the sails were hoisted the children all began to throw in the air the fireworks of sand that greet new arrivals and salute those who depart.